WHISPERS
FOLLOW ONE GIRL'S JOURNEY WITH CHRIST FROM WILDERNESS TO WHOLENESS

Kathleen Bush

Author's Tranquility Press
MARIETTA, GEORGIA

Copyright © 2022 by Kathleen Bush.

All rights reserved. No part of this publication may be reproduced, distributed or transmitted in any form or by any means, including photocopying, recording, or other electronic or mechanical methods, without the prior written permission of the publisher, except in the case of brief quotations embodied in critical reviews and certain other noncommercial uses permitted by copyright law. For permission requests, write to the publisher, addressed "Attention: Permissions Coordinator," at the address below.

Kathleen Bush / Author's Tranquility Press
2706 Station Club Drive SW
Marietta, GA 30060
www.authorstranquilitypress.com

Ordering Information:
Quantity sales. Special discounts are available on quantity purchases by corporations, associations, and others. For details, contact the "Special Sales Department" at the address above.

Whispers/Kathleen Bush
Hardcover: 978-1-958179-41-3
Paperback: 978-1-957546-69-8
eBook: 978-1-957546-70-4

Scripture quotations marked NIV are from the Holy Bible, New International Version. NIV Copyright 1973,1978,1984,2011 by Biblica, Inc.
Used by permission. All Rights reserved worldwide.

Pacific Book Review

This book tells the story of an ordinary girl who conquered the difficulties she faced to emerge as a strong independent woman at the end. Being born to a mother who was fragile and nervous and a father who faced his demons through alcohol, Kathleen grew up through a few challenges. The author takes us into two sides of her life; her personal life included family and other acquaintances and the other side of growing up in South Africa and Kenya during the colonial days. I loved how she described her journey to Kenya and how their family settled in the East African country. Even at a tender age, Kathleen had a lot of good memories while living in the country with her family.

The first chapter of the book basically talks about race riots in South Africa and the fight for independence in Kenya by the Mau Mau. One thing I liked about this book was the author had either a quote from a book or a verse from the Bible at the start of every chapter. I also observed that the quoted words were somehow related to the story that was to be told in the specific chapter. I appreciate that she did this as I am a fan of short nuggets of wisdom.

The saddest part of Kathleen's story was when she miscarried time and again. I felt sorry for her despite it happening ages ago. Her relationship with God after the miscarriages was interesting though. I love how Kathleen never gave up and continued to believe in God. I was so excited when after reading on, saw that she got to be pregnant again. I remember the words "It is a Christmas miracle Kathleen, accept it and take care of the two of you", by her doctor. I could feel how happy she was that despite all difficulties, she got the news of her pregnancy when she was five months.

Kathleen Bush has gone through a lot in life. I may not relate to everything she talked about but I sure admire her for her resilience and bravery when things went south. I enjoyed reading every bit of her life story. The author's life may not be the typical life we know, but the fact remains that one can learn plenty of lessons through her story. By reading this book, I got to understand that no one is sure of a perfect and smooth ride in this world. Life may be a rollercoaster but by trusting in God, one is able to achieve even the impossible.

It is in affliction that we find our strong points. No one knows us better than God. All we should do is trust in him as he will take care of everything. The main reason I enjoyed reading this book is that it is a light read that is full of encouraging words. Kathleen's story inspired me. Her style of writing is also excellent and easy to read. I would recommend this book to readers who have a thing for real-life stories and motivational books. You will not only be encouraged but also live the author's life through her words.

Contents

Pacific Book Review 3
Dedication 6
Preface 7
Prologue 8
Chapter 1 15
Chapter 2 28
Chapter 3 42
Chapter 4 55
Chapter 5 70
Chapter 6 88
Chapter 7 108
Chapter 8 131
Chapter 9 157
Chapter 10 165
Afterword 175
Glossary 176
About the Author 178

Dedication

This book is dedicated to the many wonderful people who have had influence in shaping my ministry as I sought to follow their spiritual imprint. None of this would have been possible without their example and that of my incredible family. Without my amazing husband of 51 years, our two handsome sons and their gorgeous children, who fill my heart with love and inspiration, Without you, I would be lost and there would be little story to tell. Thank you for believing in me and encouraging me each step of the way.

I love you.

Preface

'A traveller went on a long journey to visit a Persian mountain village where the entire population weaved splendid silk rugs that graced many palaces and noble homes, in the land. This village was unique because the skilled weavers sat at one end of the large loom and at the other end sat all the children as yet novices and young semi- skilled weavers who inevitably made many errors in the pattern and colours of the rug, along the way. No one ever pointed out their mistakes although the most gifted weaver kept one eye on what was taking place at the other end of the work. Quietly, spotting some error he would weave the mistakes into his end of the rug including them so they became part of the whole pattern and colour of the beautiful rug. Once the whole rug was complete the miracle became apparent, no mistakes could be seen only the perfection and beauty of a beautifully and perfectly woven rug, a true work of art.' Anon.

This is a metaphor for our lives. God is the master weaver who watches over our lives (our rug) and sees each error and mistake we make yet weaves these into the whole that is our life, in such a way the completed picture is one of perfection and beauty!

May each of us see and believe in the beauty that is our own in God in Christ Jesus.

So may it be.

Prologue

I was born in 1947 in Port Shepstone, Durban, Natal, (called Kwazulu-Natal today) South Africa to parents who it would seem were ill-prepared for the role. My mother was so fragile and nervous that all my nursery care was left in the hands of a young South African girl, Joy, who loved me fiercely and spoke and sang to me continuously, in her soft African voice. No wonder I grew up calling her Mumma and speaking my first words in her Bantu dialect much to my European birth mother's tremulous horror. Africa scared my mother, a fragile English rose, and she never came to make it her 'home' even after many years. She carried an elusive vision of 'home' as being a 'green and pleasant land' somewhere in England that never existed except in her imagination. If Africa represented all that was terrifying for her, England represented all that was hallowed and safe, yet the reality was something quite different. My father was the editor of the Natal newspaper and back then had a fatal attraction for alcohol which led him away from home many nights to spend time at his favourite bar. He drank, I grew up to realize, to escape the demons that the war had left behind. Deep images of death and cruelty especially of fighting in Burma (Myanmar), scarred him very deep and alcohol soothed a little of the pain. This alcoholic weakness played a part in my being named Ann Kathleen. My mother still in hospital after giving birth to me, asked my father to go and register my birth, writing down my name as Catherine Ann. My father stopped at his favourite bar before facing the official at the Birth and Deaths Registry in Port Shepstone, Durban. He stayed too long, as was normal and did not notice the paper with my names written on it, fluttering to the floor as he pulled out his wallet to settle his bill! At the Registry Office, standing before the desk of the puzzled person trying to make sense of what my father wanted, they looked at each other, eventually both agreed he was there to register his baby daughter's names and date of birth. By some miracle my date of birth was etched in his memory, his real problem only became obvious as he tried to recall the names my mother had chosen. Later he tried to explain to my angry mother, he knew Ann featured but could not remember the rest of it; after much hard guessing, eventually his beer imbibing allowed his brain to settle on Kathleen, the name of one of his sisters; Mum was not happy with him at all when she read the Birth Certificate he proudly presented her later. So Catherine Ann is forever gone and Ann Kathleen, I assuredly and legally am! My mother refused to recognize Kathleen so always called me Ann; my father always called me by his nickname for me 'Blogs', unless I was in trouble then I heard 'Kathleen Ann, oh 'tarnation! Blogs'!

This was the age of race riots in South Africa with Ghandi trying out his message of nonviolent resistance with little success. Asians and Africans fought bloody battles in the residential and commercial streets of many towns. Durban was especially unsettled having a large Asian population. My mother lived in terror convinced she would be widowed and left with me, unable to cope alone. My first memory is of my father fighting off rioters as he tried to get through our front gate into the safety of our house. He managed it, pushing someone hard before he slammed the front door shut, bolting it fast with blood pouring down his cheeks from a cut on his scalp. My mother is screaming as I look on in amazement; far too young to make sense of any of it.

My second memory is me, aged 3, on a huge (could have been small but felt huge to a tiny child) ship sailing away from Durban up the East African coast to the port of Mombasa, Kenya. I remember I felt hollow inside and so miserable, missing Joy who in truth had been like my mother, now she had left me. My daily care was entrusted to the ship's nursery which I passionately hated. I cannot remember one time of being with my parents, just the horrible nursery nurses who enjoyed corporal punishment to excess. Anything that caused them work was rewarded with a harsh pinch on the arm, thigh or buttock, somewhere not readily noticeable.

Things improved as we docked in Mombasa, Kenya and took the overnight train that pulled multi sleeper and dining carriages and baggage cars up onto the high plateau on which Nairobi, (the capitol city) was built, over 6,000ft above sea level. I loved the snug sleeper compartments with pull down bunk beds and tiny washbasins all built in and when you walked down the train to the toilet or dining carriage, it swerved and jiggled like a wriggly snake. As you came to the coupling between carriages you could look down and see the rails shining up at you and it made your tummy feel funny so I jumped over the link not trusting the open metal grid that formed the coupling plates. This part of the journey was far more fun than being on the ship. We watched the scenery change and wild animals come and go from our view. I had my parents to myself for a whole day and night. Daddy told me stories of a laughing character called 'Apple Sammy' and sang to me. Mother sat mostly silent and watchful with her anxious thoughts of this new life they hoped to live in Kenya, with no doubt a mind full of new imagined dangers on this Dark Continent.

Nairobi station was buzzing like a beehive, jostling bodies, busy and noisy, but once we got out into the city, still noise and dusty, yet all around were wondrous bursts of colour, as trees, bushes, and flowers bloomed as far as the eye settled. I loved this place immediately and excitedly bounced up and down asking over and over where we were going.

We soon arrived at our temporary accommodation, the Westland Hotel just up the hill from the Anglican Nairobi Cathedral. So many grand European style buildings to look at from the taxi window, like the vastness of the main Post Office and the iconic New Stanley Hotel. In my teenage years this became the place to be seen, our favourite hangout! Celebrities could be spotted occasionally like Robert Mitchum, here to make the movie 'African Queen'! I was to have my fourth birthday at the Westland hotel as it took many months before a house became vacant for us. But one day we left the hotel never to return and Dad drove us to our new home across the road from the European hospital. It was a three-bedroom bungalow set in a pretty garden. Jacaranda trees blazed with their spectacular purple flowers and the many hues of the bougainvillea bushes adorned the large area, with frangipani bushes and many others. I could not wait to explore each nook of this wonderland and claim it for my own. My first proper memory was when I stood with my mother at the roadside waving my little Union Jack flag vigorously as our new young Queen Elizabeth drove past in a shining limousine. Mother explained how the young queen's father had died back in England, whilst she and her new husband enjoyed a holiday in Kenya so she came to the throne as our new Queen. I wondered if she missed her father and wished he hadn't died. I could not imagine life without my daddy and his stories and songs, when he was home. The new Queen looked very young and as pretty as she waved back at us with a beautiful smile.

The roof of our new house was tin and when it rained it drowned our voices as the water drummed down. Noisily, very, very noisily! Africa was just like that to this very young Kathleen. It lured you into its heart and once you felt comfortable, it became noisy and scary so you couldn't hear yourself and felt lost and alone. It was a place I grew to love so much and yet it also scared me at times when the imaginations of evil and darkness came, usually at night, when such things threatened to take form. When I was older, I would hear adults speak of witch doctors and their dark magic and felt very scared. In the daylight, nothing much scared this girl, even the spiders hanging in their fine webs and snakes that lived in the garden.

My kind daddy built me a little wooden house in the garden in which I played for hours a make believe existence of the perfect family life, with my dolls and teddy. One evening I ran out to the playhouse trying to put off bedtime as long as possible. I think I was about 4 or 5 years old by now. As I bent down to enter the doorway, I saw my father must have placed an old black tire in the corner for me to sit in. The light was fading, dusk comes quickly in Africa, but there was still enough light to see faintly. I sat myself upon the tire, which was very warm to the back of my legs, just as I heard my father calling me in for bedtime. His voice came closer as he walked towards the playhouse knowing very well, I would be hiding in there. His face appeared in the doorway just as he lit a match to his cigarette and as the match flared, I saw his face drain chalky white. With a hand outstretched to me he quietly said *"Blogs, stay very quiet and gently get up and slowly walk over to me,*

NOW!" I knew better than to disobey that voice, so I did exactly as he said and as soon as I reached the doorway, he grabbed me in his arms and ran with me to the house calling loudly for Chumbe, our houseman to come with his gun. I was thrown in the kitchen door as Dad and Chumbe ran towards my playhouse. One shot rang out in the dusk and then Chumbe yelling excitedly reached into the little wooden house pulling on something long and black. It was almost as long as he was tall as he dragged it across the grass towards me and my startled, ever watchful mother. My father bent down to me and explained 'the tire' was in fact a very large snake which thankfully had been asleep and not bothered by my tiny body resting on its coils. He took it to show a friend at the snake park but never said more about what type it was, only that I was the luckiest girl in the world, not to have been bitten. I always wondered if it was a black mamba, an extremely deadly African snake, but whatever it was, it left me with a healthy respect and wariness about all serpents. I never played in my little house again it was spoiled for me, evermore.

This is typical of Africa, just when you thought you were on good terms, she would show another facet of her many hidden dangers and wonders. As I grew up, I learned never to take her for granted, but also never to live in fear, either. After all she flowed through my veins and I was and always have been, a child of Africa, of this wondrous, vast surprising continent the land of my birth. Looking back, I am amazed that I escaped relatively unharmed in those tender years of ignorance and foolishness. When much older, I would defy my father's strict instructions to never take the buses to the African or Asian areas of the city and never to walk down certain streets without an adult escort. They would be horror-struck if they had found out half of what I did alone and still I came home unscathed and never once was I hurt or threatened by anyone. On the contrary, I made many new friends who would wave or call out to me 'Hello little memsahib' and offer me bottles of cold coco-cola or some candies. Even some of the regular beggars came to know me by name and would refuse to accept any money I tried to offer them; somehow knowing I needed it to get the bus back home. Africa is a large part of who I am and I found its native peoples to be gentle, generous, good natured and protective of those who came with open hands and hearts. I have a deep abiding respect and love for my country of birth and the birthright given me. It has gifted me with a trust for all people until they prove otherwise and a love for those, others refuse to see or help.

Chapter 1

Love gives naught but itself and takes naught but from itself. Love possesses not nor would it be possessed; When you love you should not say, "God is in my heart," but rather, "I am in the heart of God"

-The Prophet by Kahlil Gibran

It was a perfect Kenyan morning, in all its possible glory under the African sky. Iridescent blue studded with fluffy white clouds encouraged this twelve-year old Kathleen who quietly got herself dressed and ready. I most certainly did not want to wake my mother or nosy little sister, for then all my plans would come to nothing. Thankfully, Father had already left for his golf club and wouldn't be home for hours. I hugged myself with delight and just knew that today everything would go right. This adventure had waited long enough to be put into action.

Our houseman, Chumbe, never worked on Sundays. Mum cooked our meals so he had at least one full day to himself, not that he worried me. I could always wrap Chumbe round my little finger. Chumbe would never have tried to stop me. He knew the little memsahib always got to succeed once she set her mind to something. Chumbe had served with my father in WWII in the King's African Rifles and refused to leave him once the war ended. Forevermore, he was Dad's houseboy which automatically morphed into being part of the family once Dad married. Now Chumbe looked after us all with great loving pride and patience.

Chumbe was more like a grandfather figure to me and would praise me occasionally, yet when he thought I deserved it, he would also discipline me vocally in a quaint mix of English and Swahili, which usually left me giggling. This only made him sterner and say even funnier things.

On the other hand, my mother, who had no patience with me ever, would have screeched and waved her arms, threatening me with "Wait till your father gets home." Yes, well, I would be safely back home by the time he dragged himself from the golf club bar.

Although I was considered tall for my age, I could not reach very high up in the larder but managed to score a slice of bread from the bread bin on the middle shelf. Then I scraped jam from the fridge onto the slice, with my finger. This went down easily with some water from the boiled-water jug in the fridge.

With breakfast over, I licked my fingers clean and, after making sure I had a clean handkerchief, quietly left from the back door. Jack, my sweet Alsatian, sat up eager for play. I rubbed his ears and told him to keep quiet. His eyes looked mournful. "No walk then or play even?" those soulful eyes pleaded.

"Sorry, Jack. Not this time. You must stay and be quiet. On guard!"

Always the obedient ex-police dog, Jack sat straight up on his haunches. He knew how to obey an order, unlike my little sister who had to be the most contrary person in my world.

Yes, of course, I remembered all the times my parents had sternly instructed that I should not walk anywhere alone and that I must stay within the confines of our garden! Goodness, the Mau Mau time was over several years ago, and besides, I usually took Jack with me.

During the week when not at school, I had to get out exploring. Nairobi offered so many exciting possibilities for me. I was used to walking some long distances along the Queen Elizabeth Highway, which was lined with elegant, regal jacaranda trees and rainbow colors of the bougainvillea bushes. Two miles was no distance as I easily walked to the Nairobi Museum, with its tantalizing displays of Dr. Leakey's finds of early human fossils in Olduvai Gorge on the edge of the Serengeti Plains. I spent hours happily lost in my imagination, trying to picture early humans fighting for survival in this beautiful yet harsh land.

This was my home, and I had that childlike innocence that no one would ever harm me; perhaps my ignorance helped in my protection. Harm would be done to me, but not here in Africa. It would be far away, across oceans, in years to come.

This day, I had picked a different adventure. No, that is not true in the least. I had not picked this one; it felt as though something was drawing me toward a mysterious goal. It seemed I had been selected.

For the last few Sundays as I awoke, in the pit of my stomach I had a strange, fizzy feeling of mystery awaiting discovery. The *what* of the discovery always eluded me and left me feeling as though I had failed some sort of test or quest.

The *where* was easily identified as the Anglican cathedral in Nairobi, almost one mile from where we lived. No, I could not explain with any more detail. I just knew this was where I had to go. Nothing like this had ever happened to me before!

I must explain. Although my mother on rare occasions, when she felt the need to talk about her childhood, told us children that her family back in England had been members of the Congregational Church of Wales, I never saw any evidence of her being religious. In fact, she never went to church, even at Christmas and Easter, or took us children to Sunday school.

My father never tired of telling me he was an atheist because of his wartime experiences of humanity's cruel excesses. He could no longer believe in a loving God.

Our home was devoid of any spirituality, unless my father's blaspheming words counted. So I determined this discovery was all up to me, once I was convinced the strange, urgent pull to get inside the place of God wasn't going away. I would take myself to church—and not just any church but the wondrous, huge Anglican cathedral.

Walking was my only transportation, so on this perfect Sunday morning, I slinked out of our garden and headed off down the road. I was confident, with my back straight and head up, just as my father told me all soldiers marched. I suspected he really wished I was a boy to follow in his military footsteps. "Sorry, Dad. I am a girl after all." But I tried to please him as best I could, so I marched *left, right, left* with arms swinging, determined never to skip along like a girl.

Cars drove past me, slowing down at the sight of a white female child marching along the sidewalk alone. I ignored them while looking straight ahead, and thankfully no one stopped to ask me any questions. Perhaps they too were aiming for church, this being Sunday.

Then I had a hopeful thought. *Perhaps there are others like me who are urgently pulled toward God's house. Perhaps they were catching faint whispers in the depths.* Gosh, it would be so comforting if I knew someone else was experiencing what I was.

When I arrived, I felt daunted, full of apprehension tinged with excitement. The cathedral was huge, towering above me and the surrounding car park, which was almost full.

I melded into the flow of people entering through the majestic doorway, trying to look confident and as if this was what I did every Sunday morning. In truth, I felt very small and scared. *What am I doing here? I have no idea what will happen and what I should do next.* This question was quickly answered by one of the ushers who seemed to sense I was alone. He tried to direct me toward the hall next door, where I was informed, "All the children gather for Sunday school."

"No," I tell the man, firmly looking him straight in the eye—like I guess a soldier would. "I need to stay in here." So, I progressed down the long aisle until I could slide into an empty seat. I hoped he wouldn't follow me and throw me out, but it seemed he had given up.

I looked puzzled at the array of books in front of me. What on earth were they for? Remember no Bibles, prayer books, or hymnbooks existed in my house. I was now in foreign territory.

I was soon to discover they used a very foreign language too. I jumped as the loud organ made its peremptory sound and the first hymn rang out. I had not a clue what I should be doing, and the next hour passed in an incomprehensible blur. I stood with everyone else ("Who gives the signal?" I ask myself.) and sat when they sat, but beyond that, I could not follow anything. *What is going on here? But*—oh yes, there is a *but—I feel I belong here, despite how strange it all is.* There it was again, the fizzy feeling in my stomach and such joy. I felt I was home and loved and exactly where I should be, but still without any understanding of why.

Today, I know this is called being aware of the numinous, the sense of other, the divine spirit: God. Back at only twelve years old, it reduced to being a fizzy sense in my stomach. I was in the presence of something so very special, otherworldly, and unseen yet infinitely superior to all humanity.

As soon as the service was over, I rushed out the door; thankfully the usher had disappeared.

My walk home gave me time to think over this experience, which felt so weird yet so right.

You guessed it. I arrived home to anything but a warm welcome.

My mother screeched her usual refrain, and my sister looked on with glee that I was once again in deep trouble.

When Father eventually showed up, I got the beating I had been promised and was sent to my room.

As I looked back on that day's adventure, trying not to think of my punishment, I felt something momentous had happened. I felt that a part of a bigger plan had somehow commenced but was just out of reach. I sense glimpses of something that eludes me like a whisper from deep within that is not quite audible. It is stronger than intuition yet not strictly an audible sound. What is going on? Am I going mad? Perhaps I should act like a 12-year-old and forget all about this. A week at school helps me forget. Friday evening comes around again and finds my thoughts refocused on the Cathedral. Does God live in there? Who is God anyway? Is he whispering to me? I shouldn't think so; according to my parents I am too willful and rebellious for much good. Yet I feel drawn to go back; yes, I will return on Sunday, I promise myself cheerfully. Both parents are going out for lunch and my sister is staying at a friend's house, whilst I am deemed old enough to stay home with Jack and behave myself! Great! Sunday morning sees me striding out down to the Cathedral with greater confidence this week. I know the ropes this time and will avoid the ushers by mingling with a group of adults, so they hide me in their throng until I safely pass the doorway. Today I want to sing the hymns and even pray a prayer in the silence asking God if he is there to let me know so I don't think I am mad. No voices speak my name, nothing except a stronger feeling that I belong in this place and I am welcomed. After the usual standing and sitting routine (church keeps you fit) the service ends and we all begin to leave. I am just pushing into the aisle when one of the priests (I did not know then what he is called) touches my shoulder and signals me to stand to one side. Oh, Oh! Am I in trouble? He smiles down at me and asks me for my name. 'Kathleen,' he says smiling with his whole face, in fact his face was glowing and did he have tears in his eyes? "I have watched you from the front all through the service and know you are here alone, aren't you? Oh, crumbs I thought, this is where I get into big trouble, but this kind looking man continued, "But you aren't really alone because this is your heavenly Father's house and He is all around us. I sense He has a purpose for your life and has drawn you here so I can tell you He is real and his angels will look after you because you will go out into the darkness and will walk in the shadows for a while, before coming home to where you belong. Even on the darkest days when you feel alone and scared, never forget God is with you." Wow! Questions filled my mind; I had so many to ask this kind gentle person who I sensed really knew God well. I took my clean hanky to blow my nose and wipe my watery eyes, this was most unexpected, yet I did not feel scared only puzzled. When I looked again the man had disappeared into the crowd. What had just happened was I having a waking dream? But some of the people around me must have heard what the priest said because they were smiling at me and nodding in an encouraging way that adults have towards well behaved children, one lady also wiped her eyes and quietly said may 'God bless you dear child'. Wow! What a morning, I couldn't wait to get home and digest all this. I really wished there was someone I could talk to about all of this.

You are most probably thinking that this gets better and better, but sorry to disappoint but nothing else like this happened for weeks. During the following week our school holidays began and we all set off to Mombasa to the Nyali Beach Hotel for 2 weeks glorious fun. Sorry to say, I forgot all about my experiences in the Cathedral and the whispering senses dimmed in my head and my heart. Such is the fickleness of the young, always on to the next attraction. Living in the moment!

Reflecting now in hindsight as an adult, about my response to what had been a momentous 'word' spoken by one of God's ministers, I think that at a very deep level I knew God had gotten my attention and knew somehow, He would initiate the next step, so meanwhile I enjoyed being 12/ 13 years old. I did find myself on some Sunday mornings going to other church services but never returned to the Cathedral alone and never again did any minister speak any words from God to me. It seemed His present purpose was to gain my attention towards Him, that He existed and was real. This belief never wavered although I was not to discover more about Him, for many years. I also believe He protected me and this was why I never felt threat or harm from any person or situation that others may have turned from. Angels walked alongside me when I crossed into enemy territory and kept me safe.

The decades have shown me so clearly that God my heavenly Father was opening my eyes to His love for me, that my life did have purpose and showing me His heart. The journey to this realization was to take me many painful steps into the shadows that swirled around the edges of such darkness that I almost lost me way as well as my life. However, be patient for this part of my story will unfold later in my story.

I still would awake with that fizzy feeling that on this Sunday, there should be another church visit and so I would take myself next door to our house, to St Andrew's Kirk and along the road to the Lutheran Church, but no repeats of the Cathedral experience except the knowledge I belonged in God's house, whosoever's hands built it.

Meanwhile school filled my horizons with each passing year. When I reached 13 or 14 years of age, I made a new friend, Aileen. Her father was in the military on a posting to Kenya for 2 years. I loved spending weekends with Aileen at her house where her mother made me very welcome. Her parents were very religious and I learned that people prayed before meals and went to church every Sunday without fail.

The first time I joined them at the Military Chapel on the army base I was shocked at how upbeat and informal the service was compared with what I had experienced in my brief religious incursions to denominational churches. But I soon loved it, they had a band playing the music and nobody had to stand or sit to order you did what you felt like. I also began to listen to the messages spoken by the chaplain. I learned all sorts of things about our loving God and he even had a son. But when Easter came around and I heard that God allowed His Son to die on the Cross I felt sick and very angry, this wasn't right surely. Was this what Dad meant about cruelty and why he could not believe in God? I asked Aileen and she got her mother to explain things slowly to me. When she told me that Jesus had to die but on the third day came alive again to show us that God's power is always stronger and the darkness is always overcome by His Son's light, and death has no power anymore, I remembered the priest in the Cathedral telling me I would go out into the darkness for a while, but God would still be with me. Did this mean I too had to die before God's power came? I felt scared yet also knew somehow God would never allow anything bad to happen. I kept attending Church with Aileen until her family left Kenya when their posting was up. I found it so lonely when she left, now I had no way for hearing about God and His gentle son Jesus and nobody to answer my many questions.

I tried to ask my mother, but she became embarrassed and would mumble "later Kathleen, later."

Assembly time at school was no help, I love singing the hymns and enjoyed the short prayers, even memorizing one called The Lord's Prayer which helped me feel closer to Jesus and God, but there was no message or teaching from the bible. I am writing this in my sixth decade and can still remember the hymns we sang at school and most of the words too. They have been within my memory and my heart all these years as a testimony of God's love and purpose.

Decades later, as I think of how too many schools in the west, today, no longer allow any religious spirit or instruction to be shared and children are bereft of any understanding about God just as I was in my home, I pray that a change will come and the wilderness will be allowed to blossom again with springs of living water and the word of God, and children will grow and develop in the knowledge of God and His love for them.

I thank God for Aileen and her parents who took me to the source of 'living water' and shared their faith with me for it was to be a long time before I drank from God's spring again.

Looking back, I realize how the little spiritual input from school assemblies nourished me enough so I could survive once the darkness surrounded me.

I must explain something about the Mau Mau uprising which caused terrible injuries and gruesome death to many white and Asian settlers in Kenya. Jomo Kenyatta of the Kikuyu tribe was feared by the British to be plotting an uprising to overthrow the white government. He had been educated in England and married an English girl and was a highly intelligent person who made an imposing enemy. The British arrested him and sent him into exile in Great Britain, an action that only caused the Kikuyu to become violently inflamed with deadly determination to drive all the foreigners out of their land. So, for many years they fought guerrilla warfare from their hidden camps within the Aberdare Forest on the slopes of Mount Kenya. They infiltrated households posing as house servants and then struck usually at night, stabbing and burning hundreds of the white or Asian households to death. I was too young to understand the ramifications and horror of what went on but do have memories of my father locking us in the house before he joined other men to take guard duty in our neighbourhood. He showed me at 6 years old how to handle and shoot a handgun in case our home was invaded. To this day, I have a hatred of guns and knives, and would never go hunting once I was older. It was a dreadful time and when I was old enough to read and learn the background and history of this time, it left me very sad for both sides. Jomo Kenyatta was eventually released by the British and came home to Kenya to become their first President after Independence (Uhuru) was declared in December 1963.

Our houseman, Chumbe, was a Kikuyu, and would ask my father each night to lock him into his little house so the guerillas could not get to him to turn on us. Other friends and families my parents knew were not so fortunate and lost their lives, often at the very hands that had cooked and cleaned for them. Many Kikuyu hands that had rocked the cradles of the young also slaughtered or led other killers to the same infants and children. It was a terrible time and left a dark stain that took years to fade. The stain still remains with its treacherous legacy of violence and death. Blame has to be apportioned on all sides as no one was innocent or without blood on their hands.

Chapter 2

*"Wretched and close to death from my youth up,
I suffer your terrors; I am desperate."*

- Psalm 88.15 NRSV

It is New Year, 1965 and I am about to embark on my first solo adult adventure to seek out a career in Air Traffic Control in England. School is finally over, and I managed to gain great grades in most subjects. These last years have not been particularly happy for me. I loved academic studies but hated physical sports which were enforced upon us. I am happiest with my nose in a book learning something new about this wonderful world of ours. My favourite subjects have been Science (biology, chemistry and physics) and Geography and English literature. All else was a struggle so I cannot apply to medical school as I dreamed of doing, as I failed Latin, scraped by in Mathematics. I discovered a talent for acting if only I could overcome my shyness! I excelled at Needlework, which became a lifelong hobby. My parents strongly advocated against me going to university in South Africa as the Apartheid problems were growing out of control. I did not feel ready for university anyway so we decided I would try to gain entry into the Civil Aviation Authority in England. If successful, the training would be entry level for university and my science and geography gave me secure grounding so I applied and now had to fly to England for the interview!

We sat around the supper table among the scattered empty plates, although I had fed most of my food handful by handful to Jack who sat close to my feet. He knew something momentous was happening to our family and it wasn't good! He could sense my misery as I hardly could hold back the tears. As I looked around the table hungrily scanning my parents and Jane's faces, imprinting them into my memory as if I would never see them again, I could not accept that in an hour we would leave this house and I would never return. I would never return to Kenya again. What had I done, I was scared and yet excited as my journey into adulthood was about to begin although I did not feel ready. Jack licked my feet and hands as though he was savouring my scent for the last time. Regrettably, Jack had to remain behind in Kenya and would be given into the care of one of my father's friends to live on his farm until his death some years on. We both knew we were saying goodbye. I have always hoped our pets will join us in heaven, so Jack and I will be together in eternity.

I said my goodbyes to my family at the departure gate in Embakasi Terminal (known today as Jomo Kenyatta International Airport) and prepared to board the very first commercial flight of British United Airways (BUA) Flight 001, a brand new VC10 jet airliner flying its first passengers from Nairobi to London Gatwick airport via Entebbe in Uganda. My previous flying had been in tiny training aircraft and once in a DC3! This aircraft looked massive in comparison.

As I nervously settled into my seat, I looked about the full aircraft feeling so young at only 17 and painfully out of place. This was it no chance of changing my mind. My future beckoned!

We roared down the runway then the powerful engines projected the plane into the sky like a rocket. I felt terrified as I was pushed back into my seat by the rate of acceleration. This was my first jet flight and it seemed I may not survive; surely the aircraft would break up into tiny pieces and scatter us all over the National Game Park. Angels had to be watching over us as we leveled out at the cruising altitude and headed towards the mighty Lake Victoria and Entebbe airport.

As I tried to relax in my seat, my mind took me back to a few weeks before when a group of us drove up into the Ngong Hills outside Nairobi to give me an opportunity to say goodbye to this incredible country I loved so much. The name comes from a Maasi phrase meaning *'knuckles'*, referring to the four peaks of the ridge of the Ngong Hills. The Ngongs run along the very lip of the Great Rift Valley, dropping 1000 metres to the valley floor below. Often on previous visits we had met a wizened old Kikuyu elder always dressed in tribal robes with a wood staff, who told us he was blind, his eyes were very milky maybe with cataracts? Yet he always knew who we were (the same European young people). We would usually leave him some food as he loved cookies and candies! Our Swahili did not extend to long descriptive conversations although we tried. This afternoon he was not in his usual spot close to the carpark and so we trekked along to the edge gazing out and down to the bottom of the Rift Valley; there was the extinct volcano Mt. Longonot raised up as a perfect cone from the valley floor, faintly visible in the distance. We had all climbed it together back when we were still in High School and it took huge effort. My heart was so heavy; how could I leave this land which I loved! I wiped away sad tears and we began to move back to the vehicle when I heard a voice calling softly, 'Hujambo, mumma'

; delighted, I turned around to see our elderly Kikuyu friend sitting close to where we had just walked! He was blind yet caught hold of my sleeve, no one else, and said so clearly 'Kwaheri Kathleen' meaning 'Goodbye Kathleen'. We all heard him and yet nobody had ever told him our names but maybe he heard the others call me Kathleen. On board the aircraft I knew I was to accept this as a gift, a special goodbye from the heart of Africa and I treasured this gift in my heart. Africa recognized I was leaving and the Kikuyu elder conveyed its message to me. This eased my sorrow for I felt a promise ease my sorrowful heart, that my connection with the land of my birth would never be broken.

As the plane descended to land at Entebbe airport, dusk was approaching but there was enough light for glimpses of hippopotamus playing along the Lake's shoreline and giraffe and zebra racing away across the plains from the noise of our aircraft. Touching down like a feather we taxied to the small terminal building. Our Captain informed us we all had to disembark and sit in the terminal whilst they refueled the plane to continue onto Gatwick.

The terminal was very quiet as we were the last departure of the day. I obediently swallowed my airsickness pill thinking we would be back in our aircraft seats very soon. I am one of those people who react by becoming very drowsy; stupidly, I had taken my medication way to early. As we continued to wait in the terminal, my eyes were closing, I fought hard to keep awake, no way was I getting left behind! The twenty-minute wait turned into two hours when we were all suddenly alerted by loud shouts, spotlights and sounds like gunshots coming from the runway area. It was too dark to see anything, but we were somewhat unnerved until one of our flight attendants reported that live monkeys had escaped their cages as they were being loaded onto our aircraft. The shipping handlers had forgotten to sedate them first. It must have looked very funny if only we could have seen, monkeys scrabbling all over the place trying to avoid capture a second time, and who could blame them? Soon they all were back in their cages, sedated and we too were loaded; I was much sedated and could hardly climb the steps to find my seat. I fell asleep before the aircraft even moved and only awoke when the smells of breakfast filled the cabin. Looking out of my window I saw the mighty rose-tinted Atlas Mountains spread majestically below, rising out of the desert sands which rolled on as far as one could see. My final sight (for over another 35 years) of the African continent was spread beneath me.

Gatwick airport in Sussex, was dismal, throngs of people, loud and bullying as each pushed their way through to be first in whatever queue they headed for. Finally, I broke free to be received into the welcoming arms of my mother's two best friends Jay and Kay in the vast Arrival Hall. I felt completely safe for the first time since I had hugged Jack back at home. Home? Where would I be calling home from now on? Anxiety crept up like a wet woolly blanket threatening to smother me. The shadows were moving towards me ever closer. I did not like this feeling or this place, called England one bit. Why had I wanted to leave Kenya?

The next few days passed me by in a jetlagged blur as I shopped for an interview outfit, juggled with a new currency and painfully tried to befriend London's underground (metro) system. Every person was in such a hurry and I was swept along with them in whatever direction the tide took me. One needed to be alert and know exactly where you were going and where you needed to be in advance. I had several unscripted arrivals until I got the hang of the subway map.

Jay and Kay were kind and encouraging but wisely left me to work things out as I struggled to find my place.

The day of my interview finally arrived and I was on my way to the Civil Aviation House at The Adelphi. Arriving much too early, I watched the changing of the Guard at Horse Guards Parade nearby. It raised my spirits to see the colourful marching columns of Guardsmen, keeping perfect rhythm to the Regimental Band in the bright morning sunshine with the traffic noise of London ever present behind us. All nerves settled down and I left to find the place for my interview.

This morning, I could have done with a few whispers from God but He was silent. Or was He? Somehow the interview ended positively, despite my best efforts to ruin my it by dropping my gloves under the chair I was sitting on and looking most undignified as I scrabbled about to pick them up. Looking up to see the panel of interviewers frowning at me as if I had brought a bad smell into the room with me, I began to tremble softly and fought the desire to flee. Yet soon I calmed and answered every question with confidence and clarity. This had to be God's peace.

By the grace of God, I passed! I was accepted and offered a place on the next training course at the Air Traffic Control College, Hurn Airport in Bournemouth. This was the reason I found myself on the train from London's Waterloo Station to the south coast as my life journey began in earnest in March 1965. Amazing to look back and trace the path of God placing us in our correct positions. For me this meant being on course to meet my future husband and all that would bring. But I had no idea of what the future held for me at this time. The shadows were encroaching as homesickness spawned it painful seed. Bournemouth seemed grey, vast and unknown and threatening to swallow me up. The Bed and Breakfast House booked for my stay at Hurn College had not reserved a room for me but the manager blithely told me I could share with another girl as he knew of no vacancies in other B&BS the area. My angels had taken flight and were nowhere to be found as I unhappily climbed the long steep stairs to the attic level of the house to find my 'shared' bedroom. What the manager had forsaken to tell me was I also shared the double-bed!

My darkest time was yet to come but this felt bad enough thank you. I loved the training course and committed myself to studying extraordinary subjects all hidden in mystery to me until now, navigation and metrology, Air Law, Rules of the Air etc. I rejoiced in this new world that opened before my eyes as my 'personal' life disintegrated into a kind of hell. My roommate, free from her aged parents for the first time, was determined to enjoy a full hectic romantic life and had little interest in the study of Air Traffic Control. Many evenings I had to sit on the stairs to study as she enjoyed getting to know her new male friend in our bedroom. Here was I, still a virgin and a really ignorant virgin at that, enduring 12 weeks of sheer embarrassing misery, almost each evening and weekend.

It was whilst sitting out on my stair I drew on the memory of the priest's words to me in the Nairobi Cathedral and tentatively called out to God ..." help me please!" To my remorse, the stairwell remained deadly silent, cold and unwelcoming as the noisy lovemaking rallied loudly through the bedroom door.

God, it seemed had left me alone. Had those striking wondrous feelings and inspiration back when I was younger just been my imagination? Perhaps it had all been a cruel charade at the expense of a lonely, naïve, little girl. I felt so alone at that moment, believing even God had given up on me. My stair became my torture chamber as I allowed myself to sink deeper and deeper into puzzled despair that adults had patronized and lied to me about a distant, fickle if not nonexistent God as a child, which added to my frustration that then became anger then threatened to morph into white hot rage. I managed to stop before the rage took over and channelled my anger, so it began to fuel my energy for hard determined study. Determination to excel on the course and I graduated with top marks of 96% much to my older classmates' chagrin. I also made a promise to never allow any adult to ever patronize me again, my protective armour fitted snugly, and no soft emotion could reach me now. Popularity did not attract me one bit, if God did not exist then I would handle my life alone. I made an inner vow, to never allow anyone imagined or real to mean anything to me. What a sad figure I was at 17 when I should have been carefree and full of hope and romantic joy, but nobody could tell me as my mind was made up. I devoted all my efforts to me newfound aviation career, having no interest at all in romance or fun. Instead, insecurity, low esteem and shyness grew ever more persuasive as slowly I lost sight of who I had been.

Of course, I was feeling the ugliness of homesickness and my shyness meant I spent far too much time alone, but with no parents to guide me I shuffled through the days and nights as best I could in my ignorance and immaturity. My mother's brother lived close with his family and became a saviour appearing regularly to take me for dinner and let me talk out my frustrations whilst on the course. Freshly out of the college I was posted to London Heathrow Airport and made my new home in shared accommodation at the Women's Hostel. My room mates were lovely and became good friends, but they had their own lives and careers and the support of families for home visits. Without my family, I began to take new tracks on my journey of life, as the desire to learn grew in me devouring me so there was no energy or time for anything frivolous or fun. I determined to test new waters to see if God existed in some other corner I had yet to discover. I read all books I could find on the great world religions, visiting temples and other places of worship, always alone, but none offered anything that grabbed hold of my mind or my heart. I learned a lot and met some gentle, kind people, devotees of this religion and that but could never be convinced that they truly had found the way to God or at least not God as I sensed Him to be back in earlier years. I was becoming despondent, yet driven, there had to be some trail, some clue waiting for me to find it. Mixed into my quest was beginning my career at London Heathrow Airport. Few young women worked in Air Traffic Control back then in the late 1965. I found it very difficult to make friends and truly preferred my own company and my books. When cajoled to come out of my shell and join in the 'fun', I counted the hours until I could return 'home' to the Hostel. Fun as others around my age seemed to enjoy, eluded me but I did have a few friends who despite my shyness and quiet ways were loyal and understanding. What an awkward, odd young woman I must seem to onlookers?

Having exhausted my exploration of world faiths, without any idea of how vulnerable I was, I took a very dangerous step towards real darkness and began to search facts out about the occult. It scared me and yet I felt drawn like a magnet, I never ventured beyond reading about it, thankfully. I began to have terrible nightmares; anxiety overcame me for no reason, my insecurity and shyness grew worse. I knew I shouldn't read these books but stupidly I kept on whilst so aware of an inner whisper, to turn away; turn away now before I stepped in any deeper. One night having met an old friend from Africa for supper in central London, I was returning back to the Hostel close to Heathrow on the last tube/subway train for the night; this meant changing trains at Barron Court metro station; being the only person waiting on the platform I sensed someone was looking at me trying to catch my attention; as I looked around I saw standing in a darkened corner, face in shadows, a tattered old coat, undone buttons almost covering a semi naked male figure, his face remained in the shadows but his very obvious 'male genitalia' held in one hand was being vigorously waved in my direction. All breath left my lungs as I began to tremble, helpless and traumatized as I imagined this person coming closer. Thankfully, he didn't move towards me but remained in the half shadows until my train arrived within minutes. My first prayer ever prayed in real earnest, was that he does not enter my train and that I get home safely. This prayer was honoured to my endless thanks. This left me feeling shaken, very vulnerable and scared. I shared this incident with my friends who laughed it off and said why let it affect me so much, he never touched me or harmed me, did he? But he did harm me, because he stirred up a long buried memory of someone else that had sexually molested me and scarred me, but I couldn't tell them that. In today's world of open, frank sexual dialogue and information this would have not been a regarded a very big deal at all, but for me it was terrifying, for it pulled a scab off a deep wound, leaving it wide open in all its nastiness. When I was 9 years old, my parents left me for a few hours with an elderly male relative who did the same to me (exposing his naked private parts) as he cornered me in the kitchen. He then pushed me ahead of him and sexually assaulted me; before this assault, I had innocently thought I could trust him as he was related to my mother. With hindsight he had been grooming me for a while with special treats, extra pocket money and toys. After this assault he repeatedly told me I was a very bad girl and had made him do this to me and if I ever told anyone, especially my parents or teachers, I would be taken to prison by the police. I know now this is standard paedophile behaviour towards their young victims. Despite being desperately scared, traumatized and painfully violated I believed him as he bullied me saying over and over, he had all the power over me. I dare not utter a word to my parents although I hoped they would notice my terror but they did not. No rescuer came. This occurred not just the once and left me with lasting insecurities towards sexual behaviour and adult male figures, especially those in authority. So I buried this deep within until this wretched man on the station platform dredged it all back up to the surface. This would hamper my marriage relationship for years until I sought help for psychological healing, as I always held something back, never completely able to trust or relax with my loving, gentle husband.

Yet every cloud has an unseen benefit and through this adult miserable encounter I began to sense clearly for the first time that good and evil existed in the world; we have freedom of choice as to where we step and where we focus our interest as we live our lives and where we place our trust. I could clearly understand for the first time that my choices had recently taken me so close to where evil hid in the darkness and knew I had to take responsibility for this just as I had for what I chose to do next. Determined, I took firm steps to renounce and to turn my back on all interest in the occult. Thankfully before I crossed the line and came up against real danger, all my books about occult matters I burned and I turned away for good, pleading with the Lord if he was real, to cleanse me and forgive me all wrongdoing.

A word of warning to any who are as naïve as I was back then, for what I did not know was how the darkness seeps within and can take root even when we no longer feed it by paying attention. It would be many years later until I learned the damage already done had to be rooted out of me by powerful prayers. Until this happened, the effects continued to trouble me, like a recurring spiritual, viral infection. This manifested itself through in all manner of ways, insecurities, fears, making poor choices, financial worries, and premature death of loved ones. Systematically, I was robbed of my confidence and security, until I literally saw and accepted 'the Light, Jesus Christ' and chose to live by the path of Christ's healing and redemption. When we either in ignorance or willfully follow anything that is not of Christ, seeds may be left within our minds to fester, these will eventually grow until they make their presence felt in very unpleasant ways. It makes sense such as these have to be uprooted and thrown out; bound and discarded for all time. We cannot serve two masters; all of us have to choose, either God in Christ or his enemy the devil who roams this world like a ravenous lion seeking to devour. I know now what I could not know then that love casts the strongest light, one that exposes and repels the darkness. Perfect love really does cast out all fear! Those blessed with being raised in Godly homes are nurtured in this love, yet God did not leave me alone in the dark. He was always with me even when I did not recognize Him. He nurtured me as my parents could not. Then He blessed me with a partner who would nurture my heart and cherish me.

This amazing love was waiting for me in the heart of a co-worker, one of the few young, unattached men in Air Traffic Control. We probably would not have met if I had not caved to persuasion and gone along to a birthday party at which God definitely had an agenda. Remember my earlier commitment or inner vow to never allow anyone to get close to me? In the face of God's plans all our fears and vows dissemble as I found love shining through the eyes and heart of the dearest young man, who was to become my husband, Gordon. With his unconditional love and kindness showering down on my sad life I thrived like a plant denied water. The sun shone again for me as I was nourished and cared for by this gentle darling man. He has to be one of the most patient men on earth as he so gently allowed me to slowly unfreeze and come to life again. Remember the girl who had promised herself to never trust anyone? Well this girl found the man who overcame such foolishness and persisted in his love until her/my heart melted. Do not misunderstand me, over the intervening years we both had to work at our marriage and had times of arguments and differences of opinions, but we always agreed on one thing that was to uphold the marriage vows we made together before God. This kept our marriage sacred.

My healing began its slow process, after I set my face against the pull of darkness and now anything was possible with God on my side.

Chapter 3

"Why are thou cast down, O my soul? And why art thou disquieted in me? Hope thou in God; for I shall yet praise him for the help of his countenance.

-Psalm 42. 5 KJV

On October 1st 1966 we were married on a sunny, windy day, beneath an azure sky in Hounslow, Middlesex. Neither of us could claim a family connection to any church for we did not attend. Yet God again was present directing us to "know" and to agree we had to exchange our marriage vows before Him in a sacred building. We both agreed wholeheartedly that we wanted to be married in a Christian church and chose Holy Trinity in Hounslow West. Again, God had to be in this for the Vicar, Reverend John Carter was generously patient with us as he led us through marriage preparation. He listened to my story of responding to God nudging me back in Nairobi and encouraged us to be committed to following Christ. On discovering Gordon had never been baptized, Reverend Carter insisted this rite of passage had to be completed before he married us. Gordon was not of the same mind and proved fairly resistant, but the good reverend won the day in some style! Gordon not only was baptized but also confirmed all in one service at no other than the historical gem of St Paul's Cathedral in London. The then Dean of the Cathedral heard Gordon make his baptism promises and named him before God in Christ,

Gordon Leslie, as the baptism waters dripped down his face and head. I suspected tears also flowed, I know mine did as I looked on with joyful pride at my soon to be husband, tinged with a little envy as I wished I too could be confirmed here. My confirmation was however yet to come. Reverend Carter was to be the human catalyst, so instrumental as we began our marriage in God's sight; he spiritually prepared us for the long journey ahead, so we had resources as we slowly took one step closer to making our own confession of faith years later.

My parents had returned to England from Nairobi and were now living in the Cotswolds. The months leading up to our wedding brought me closer to my mother as we shared the wedding preparation with joyous hearts. Little did I know this was to be an extremely precious time as her forty-two-year-old body was a ticking time bomb of cancer cells spreading their own insidious toxic darkness like stealth bombers. Thankfully we planned the happy day in complete ignorance and at last the day arrived, with Mum still in seemingly good health. She loved Gordon and kept telling me how fortunate I was to be his wife. Truthfully, I had no qualms, no last-minute nerves, just excitement to become Gordon's wife. Later, he told me he felt nervous enough for both of us. He looked so handsome and poised as I slowly walked towards him down the long church aisle on my proud father's arm. I just wanted to run into Gordon's arms and to never leave them. I knew my father to be very protective of me and also, he trusted me to usually make well thought out decisions. When Gordon asked him for permission to marry me, my father replied, 'please take her off my hands and best of luck to you.' Gordon knew he was joking, especially when Dad skillfully questioned Gordon about his future plans for us both. Gently yet resolutely I grew into our married life. With hindsight, I see how young and immature I must have been, but love carried us through all our failings. We both worked shift work, but not the same shift, at Heathrow Airport so we often spent individual time alone. Gordon was a very dutiful son to his divorced mother always having something to do for her when I was at work. I would spend my solo time enjoying the tourist delights of Windsor along with the many alluring shops and boutiques. I spent the hours improving my sewing and dressmaking skills as I added to my wardrobe. Our days flowed on in happiness and peace as we learned to become a couple and I slowly discovered the unique role of being a wife under the constant tenderness of Gordon's love. Like all newlyweds, we endured and survived times of tension and argument, remembering never to *'go to bed angry with each other"!*

Looking back, it seems so strange, to see how God was woven into the very fabric of our lives and yet we had such little sense of Him. I had given little thought to those early whispers in my heart when I would be led to different churches in Nairobi. I do not recall sharing any of this with Gordon as we settled into our married relationship. Yet, now writing this I sense so strongly God's presence, breathing into each new experience creating an invisible matrix of holy love, strength and caring that we would only become aware of much later in our life together.

We shared our delight in working within aviation, I still with Air Traffic Control and Gordon now with a large British airline, both working long shifts. When we did have time off together, we enjoyed walks along the River Thames, picnics in the summer or visiting family. I read a lot whenever I had time alone and was finding many popular Christian authors, inspirational.

Although, it had been important to marry in God's church we rarely discussed this afterwards and neither of us ever felt drawn to a Sunday morning worship service. Religious belief was ignored certainly never spoken about and the whispers within my heart quietened down.

Our excitement went into high gear on the day Gordon was accepted for an aviation position in Doha, Persian Gulf. We were both eager for a new adventure and my imagination was filled with desert sunsets, camel rides and getting far away from English rainstorms! I almost had finished the packing of our little apartment when what then was named the 'Six Day War" began between Israel and the Arab world. It lasted much longer than six days, and devastated relationships between the west and Arab peoples for decades. It also devastated our plans as Gordon's job disappeared and I found myself sad and depressed as I unpacked. However, now with hindsight, I sense this experience was sowing seeds for the future. Being young and resilient, we bounced back from our disappointment and Gordon decided to leave aviation and try out being a British policeman **'bobby'**, in Her Majesty's Constabulary! Perhaps our 'rose tinted spectacles' needed a polish because this was the beginning of years of sorrow and strain! The first hurdle arose with his police posting to a Market town in Buckinghamshire, when we went to inspect the police house allocated to us. It was cold, damp and cheerless with cement floors and heated by one open fire in the sitting room. When winter came, upstairs had frost inside the windows each morning and our breath looked like steam coming from our mouths as we shivered to race to get dressed before frostbite set in!! We had little money to buy furniture or drapes and linens, thank goodness for the generosity of both our parents who helped by buying most essentials for us. Whatever we placed within the house it still looked and felt dismal. I longed for Kenya so much in this time and knew homesickness all too well. It was truly dismal and this was to be our home for the next three years. We struggled with so much adversity and change, this put a great strain on our marriage. We were both so unhappy, Gordon disliked his choice of career and I resented having to leave mine behind. I had never known poverty being raised in a household that was not wealthy but always comfortable. With only one low wage, poverty became a reality and it hurt. I felt very ungracious about what our lives had become, it was all too easy to blame each other. Inevitably, we lost sight of the intimate closeness and ability to laugh at ourselves as fun flew out the window. We somehow endured those years by remembering we had made vows to each other before God **'for better, for worse; for richer and for poorer,'** and we would not allow anything to come between us. We covenanted to stand together closer than before and resolved to endure these worst times as one, until the better times returned, believing they would and so they did in God's time. We learnt a lot about each other and ourselves, somehow by God's wonderful grace we stayed committed to our marriage vows. This is a time when that matrix of God's presence was strong around us, holding us in place, keeping us true to each other, even when other things tempted us. Our second Christmas (1967) was approaching in the police house and I tried as best I could to make it look festive and cheerful with a Christmas tree and decorations, filling the house with the tantalizing aroma of Christmas baking, especially as my parents were coming for Christmas Day. I wanted to show off my new wifely homemaking skills, but nothing could disguise the miserable state of our house.

Just before Christmas Eve, I had visited our doctor, feeling nauseous and tired and had heard the greatest news that we were to become parents ourselves in early October 1968.No house defects or lack of money could dampen my spirits now. I was so happy and smiled like the preverbal Cheshire Cat! Gordon just looked scared! He was happy but realistic in the worries of another mouth to feed but kept this to himself.

Christmas Day dawned so cold inside our house unless one remained toasting toes close to the open fire in the sitting room! My parents arrived bearing many gifts, all so welcome and appreciated. One thoughtful gift from Dad was a large powerful fan heater that gave a boost in the warmth to the dining room and sitting room. The four of us enjoyed my first ever attempt at cooking a turkey and all the trimmings. Luckily my mother (a wonderful cook) helped me and had brought many goodies to supplement my larder. We heartily toasted the news of my pregnancy which had overjoyed my parents. Best Christmas gift they could have been given each remarked with glistening eyes. My mother became very quiet yet denied anything was bothering her. As they were leaving, I helped her on with her coat and noticed for the first time her belly was swollen and rounded. Normally my mother was a very slight, slim woman. As she caught me looking, she shrugged it off by laughingly saying, 'look at me I am trying to keep up with you with my own pregnant belly'! She refused to be drawn by any questions and they soon drove away to their home near Cheltenham. My early days of pregnancy passed along very smoothly, but apart from phone calls and letters I did not see my parents for a couple of months. Then one morning I received *'the call'* from Dad telling me Mum was in the hospital and we should visit as soon as we could. He refused to say anymore which meant my mind created all kinds of horrors. My mother never mentioned any illness when she wrote and being only in her 40s should have been healthy. On arrival at the convalescence home to which she had been moved the day before, she looked no worse than at Christmas, although thinner and pale. I sent my husband and father outside so we could talk uninterrupted.

Mum denied anything life threatening, she had to have an ovarian cyst removed, hence her enlarged tummy at Christmas, she laughingly explained and there were some complications, but she assured me that she would soon recover. I asked to see her surgical scar (always curious as to how medicine and surgery worked!) I was so shocked to see her long surgical wound had been drawn together and sutured with huge black sutures like kids do the first time they try to sew a seam. I knew no surgeon would have sutured her wound so carelessly if they expected her to recover and live long. I tried hard not to show my shock and soon after made my sorrowful goodbyes.

Once back in my parents' home, I challenged my father. Why had he not called me sooner when mum first needed surgery and why was each of them keeping the truth from us? Dad tried to play innocent, but I was having none of it and eventual wore him down to spill out the truth. My mother had terminal cancer and not long to live! They both hoped to spare me worry being pregnant so had chosen to keep me unaware of the truth as long as possible. I was furious with him, but my parents had always kept us 'out of the know' when they considered it best for us. I shouted at him, that I was an adult now and deserved to be treated as one. I learned my sister had not been told either although she lived at home. Jane and I had a very traumatic, tearful conversation that night. She, as disbelieving and shocked as I had been, hearing the dreadful news. We drove back home in misery and disbelief. Fragile as my relationship with my mother had always been I did love her very much and had hoped when I became a mother, we could deepen the bonds and true friendship might develop. It was to be a bittersweet few months going back and forth to visit, always waiting for the dreaded phone call from my father. Outwardly, I blossomed as my pregnancy developed. Yet felt so heartsick at what the future meant for my poor mother, and sad that our child would not ever know her. My mother knitted several items for her unborn grandchild always in blue, saying she 'knew 'it would be a boy'! She was absolutely right and sadly died 2 months before our little son was born. Her knitting was not wasted!

James was a gorgeous baby, long dark lashes feathering huge blue eyes and the sweetest little face. He had this deep chuckle that would erupt out of him if certain noises or songs pleased him. At a few months old his favourite song contained the words **"Goodness gracious great balls of fire"**! It made him chuckle so much with a lovely smile on his face. James did nothing by halves, he either laughed or cried, life was to be approached full on and he has never changed. He has never been lazy, and has a strong work ethic. From very young, he was quick to learn, extremely intelligent, out of diapers and walking before he reached his first birthday. He grew up delighting in dismantling anything mechanical which became costly as he had no interest in putting them back together again! He was born two months before my 21st birthday in December 1968. I don't think he has any memory of being the star attraction at my party on the coldest December in living memory. At least having our home crowded with friends and relatives made it seem warmer inside than usual. I desperately missed my mother and was to soon realize that until after James was safely born, I did not allow myself to feel any grief for her death. But grief does not take kindly to being kept in the shadows and was to pounce all too soon and make my life miserable for years. It was like a light being taken from me; smothering darkness fell and threatened to take over. Of course, my frail, tenuous attempts to turn to God had no structure or foundation of faith so I felt so empty and alone during this time. I would be fine for days and then just when I could breathe again this cloud of anxiety and panic would sweep over me and I felt I was drowning in quicksand. Oh, I fought it as best I could but felt overwhelmed on many occasions. Looking back, Gordon was my beloved sanctuary, my rock, so maybe he was God's agent to keep my equilibrium? He never chided me or patronized me; never told me to get a grip; to see someone or to buck up! He just loved me and offered practical help when he could, taking over James' night feeds so I could rest. He was always my companion and support. Looking back he kept me alive during the darkest times of my grief, by the strength of his love and his gentleness and kindness. In 1968 little was known about post-partum depression, but I believe that is what I suffered. Those months were hard, but they passed eventually and joy shone again as we watched our little boy grow so handsome and interested in all around him. Today, I can say our marriage was truly a match made in heaven. Praise God! But we still had to work at keeping it strong and secure. Our baby son James completed us as a family, but I carried such sadness because my mother never lived to hold him and see his beautiful smile, although she spoke so knowingly about us having a son so maybe she knew far more than we can ever imagine. I was thankful I did not go out to work and could spend my days raising our son. He was much loved as our first-born child and is always our precious elder son in whom we are so proud. He and I had a very strong bond in those early years and went everywhere together. He even had me helping with cooking classes and listening to reading at his elementary school, as he loved seeing his mother during the school day which was something I could do so gladly. Looking back as writing this book is forcing me to do, I see myself back then, in my twenties, longing to find my place as a wife and mother, yet feeling adrift. My relationship with my sister fell apart after Mum died and I had no emotional energy left to help my dear father with his own grief and guilt. He was to come and live with us eventually until his death a decade later, but for now he appeared and then disappeared from our lives, like a ghost. He was a broken shell, a shadow of a man who had never admitted to himself or to my mother the depth of his love for her nor his need of her. Why do we withhold what is really important from our dearest ones, denying so much of the love we carry within? How beleaguered we are by our own failings and weakness, especially in giving and receiving love, without the strength that comes of having faith in our God. My atheist father and his daughters who had never been nurtured or shown how to make time or room to recognize the sacred in our lives, now struggled, disabled and isolated from the ultimate One who gave us life. The last I heard from my sister is she too had followed the cold, clinical path of atheism with her husband. I pray for her so often to find her destiny, in the presence of her Creator, and to find pure joy and happiness along with deep peace.

I could not have articulated this back then, but now I stand on the other side having made my home in the heart of my beloved heavenly Father, the one who kept encouraging me with whispers, gently drawing me closer, I can see how lost I was once, and how frighteningly easy it would have been to have lost everything along with my life.

In these days of such grief, life seemed monochrome and jagged and even the love of my precious husband brought no lasting relief, no softening. Each day, the sun rose yet never shined for me. Each morning I uttered the prayer for God to get me through the hours of another day. I was going through the motions for James' sake. This dearest little boy of ours deserved better, so any energy I could offer went to him. I recall weekend trips to the zoo, making picnic lunches; trips to the seaside where we built sandcastles and ate ice creams. Yet all the time I felt numb as though there was a veil between me and fun and living. Grief is all pervading, swallowing your ability to laugh or to enjoy anything at all. I cannot imagine what Gordon really thought of me in this dreary time, but he was always beside me, caring, encouraging, loving never judging, never telling me to buck up, just being there. My steady rock who loved me back into the world. James was three years old when we afforded to go on a week's holiday to the seaside. We drove to the Kent coast in our old used vehicle and eventually arrived at the gates of the Holiday Camp! To our horror it had barbed wire fencing around the Camp; was this to keep others out or us inside, we wondered? Once inside and checked in it we discovered it wasn't too bad and had lots of activities for all ages and access to a broad white sandy beach. We spent our days keeping James amused on the toy train and swings; playing on the beach, making many wondrous sandcastles, paddling in the freezing waters of the English Channel. One evening the adult entertainment was billed as 'The Beauty Contest'. Gordon persuaded me to dress up and take especial care with my make-up and hair for the evening. I kept telling him that I would not enter any Beauty Contest, feeling very inadequate. He persisted in making us join others in the entertainment lounge whereupon I discovered he had entered me for the contest. As I threatened to leave and go to our chalet, I was urged by the Compere to come forward, and the contest began. There were six contestants all about my age (23-24 years old) some married, others single. Unbelievably, I got through to the Final and then to my utter amazement my name was being called as the winner for the week! My prize was a cheque (if I recall it almost covered our week's holiday cost) and some beauty products. I learned the contest was underwritten by Max Factor and I was invited to go to London for a national Beauty Contest in three months' time. I refused to go; this way of life was definitely not for me but had been some fun on holiday at least!

James' was around four years old, when we decided to try for another baby. I had such a healthy pregnancy with James and hoped another child would give me a return of my former easy joy and allow my laughter to bubble freely again, a healing return of the joys of the gift of life. How easy it seemed to make this choice as if it would be our decision alone. Little did we know more pain lay ahead, before we would have any return of joy. It is a good thing God only shows us the road one step at a time; we could not bear the burden of knowing more. Jesus says in John's gospel, **"in this world, you shall find trouble"**; never a truer word was spoken. My aunt had a saying "the darkness always deepens just before the dawn". It is true. I know I experienced something like this, as the dawn in all its fiery splendour took a long time to show itself to me! Ahead, there was still a dark, rocky road to travel for me, before I knew I was to find home in the dawning light again. However, Jesus also says he will help us bear the weight of our burdens, and I found this to be so true.

In the intervening years, Gordon had left the Police and returned to aviation where he was so much happier.

Chapter 4

"For I know the plans I have for you, declares the Lord, plans to prosper you and not to harm you, plans to give you hope and a future."

- Jeremiah 29: verse 11; NIV

Today, I carry this scripture in my heart; it keeps me afloat on difficult days and has become my capstone, a constant reminder that God is my strength and courage, my defender in times of trouble; however first I had to meet the God who spoke these words and He was still waiting for me to recognize him. The whispers still had to materialize into reality. Hindsight whispers to me that this scripture was always my capstone and gave my life stability even when I did not know it.

I won't tarry over the next two years or so, sufficient to say I quickly became pregnant but after 2 or 3 months I miscarried, time and time again. Looking back, I cannot tell you how I survived the heartache each loss caused me. I think my feelings, and emotions had sunk into a deep place somewhere within. I just existed day by day, often only hour by hour. Eventually, our family doctor suggested I try out the innovative fertility treatment protocol which in the early 1970s was very new and I had read of many mothers giving birth to multiple babies. Yes, we decided; Give it a go! But although all signs showed I responded well I never became pregnant during the treatment period. On a summer's morning, Gordon and I will never forget the visit to the obstetric specialist, we fully were prepared for him to stop the fertility treatment but not prepared to be told: ***"No More Pregnancies at all ever! You will never carry a viable foetus to term"***, he baldly exclaimed! His advice was we should go home, enjoy our one son and turning to Gordon he said ***"buy Kathleen a dog, to fulfil her maternal inclinations!"*** At these words, we found ourselves out in the waiting area, stunned and disbelieving. What just happened? Why no babies ever? How come James was so easy and textbook? Busy doctors don't waste time on explanations; tell it like it is and on to the next patient. Case closed for Kathleen. I was speechless and felt cheated and angry and hollow.

On getting home I clutched James to me, feeling a fierce surge of love and protection. Then began the nightmares and daily fears that something would happen to him and he would be lost forever. I would not let him out of my sight and had to keep checking he and his friend were still safe. Thankfully, he wasn't a boy who roamed far from home and happily played in our garden or his friend's up the street. Years later, I came to understand all this was part of the pathology of unresolved, chronic grief but nobody told me, nobody offered any help. Only Gordon who unconditionally kept giving out his common sense and wonderful love, my husband alone, kept me going. Friends tried to help with kind words that sounded so empty to my ears and life went on, with my world enclosing me like a bubble. I was in the world, within the bubble yet not part of the world. Oh, I went through all the motions, shopping, cleaning, cooking, loving my family yet always feeling a layer existed between me and all activities no matter how trite or important they were. Unknown to us God was about to unfold His plan.

One sunny evening Gordon had taken our boisterous Golden Retriever, Bozwell (abbreviated to Boz by the family) for a walk down to the village (yes, we took the doctor's advice and bought our gorgeous pup. He truly helped me somewhat as dogs cannot exist in a bubble, at least Boz filled my days with unconditional loving attention of the most exuberant kind and from time to time I felt actually real again!) on his return from being dragged behind Boz, Gordon told me that he had met up with an ex-police colleague who had just moved his family to our village, on a transfer. This family had been very good neighbours when we all lived in those damp grim police houses. Jenna made a wonderful friend and they had four lovely daughters. How great to be able to renew our friendship. Little did I know but God was about to gain my attention once more and Jenna was one of his angels, I am sure. Jenna sat listening to me tell her of my experiences with trying to get pregnant, over coffee. It had never been a problem for her hence four children, but she did not come out with the normal platitudes I usually had to endure, like *'at least you have one child'* or *'you could adopt and give an orphan child a loving home'*. Thankfully Jenna had more sensitivity than most other people and just listened empathetically. When I ran out of steam and tears, she hugged me before having to rush off to her family. I didn't mind, it had felt good to talk all the painful incidents out of my system, then it hit me, this was the first time I felt this way and it felt very good, maybe even hopeful. The next day, I was slightly surprised to see Jenna again approach my door, looking a little hesitant. There was an uncertain note in her voice as she explained she couldn't stay for a visit today but wanted to lend me a precious book, which she urged me to read. It seemed awkward for her to ask if I had any faith in God and since no reply instantly fell from my lips, she hurried on to say she and her family were all Christians and church goers and this little book had helped her when her mother died and helped another friend who had experienced multiple miscarriages too. All I heard were the words 'when her mother died', so I grabbed the book, thanked her and quickly closed the door. With the door behind me I slid to the floor hugging the book to my chest with tears running down my face, thinking 'no book can possibly help me, this is rubbish'! At the same time I desperately wished it could help me. I was such a mess of hurt, yet paradoxically had hope with a burning desire for healing. Yet I was so cynical and dismissive of what I thought of as 'quick fixes.' What would I give for a way through all this mire? Certainly not my life, I wanted life in all its fullness, I craved it for us, our family. The book seemed to burn into my chest forcing me to hold it up in the air and so to be able to read the cover. I barely took in the title, something about **"God does answer prayers because He loves You"**. Since I did not have a clue how to pray this book was useless to me or so I first thought. I put it my bedside drawer, with every intention of giving it back unread next time I saw Jenna. I was way beyond books, or so I thought! Yet something deep within had unlocked, there was an easing in my heart, a spark that had not been present before. Words spoken by Reverend Carter during our wedding preparation kept coming into my mind however hard I tried to ignore them. He had told us the story of the Prodigal Son and of the raising of Lazarus from the dead among others but these stuck there prompting me to explore them again. I had a small bible he had given Gordon on his Baptism, so I searched for these stories and found them and so many others. These gospel accounts suggested a supernatural power was at work for those who believed in God and His Son; a power that worked miracles beyond human endeavours. If God was real, then surely he could help us as well. But in fairness why should he want to help me? Jenna seemed to believe he could otherwise why lend me her book? How did one gain such belief in God? My experience suggested God believed in me, yet I did not know Him at all (yet!). I needed help with this dilemma!

Something important was developing in my broken heart; a softening as if in preparation for a momentous event. Then the 'old fizzy feeling in my stomach returned'; this was familiar. I remembered this sensation all too well and welcomed it back like a long-lost friend. One night later that week unknown to us, God set the scenario. Gordon had to cover a night shift as someone had called sick and I was left alone with James who slept well once he eventually got to sleep. I hated being alone at night during this time, but at least I had Boz as company. We lived in a bungalow, so all rooms on one level, with large windows that opened by swinging outwards. Normally Gordon always checked the windows were all tightly closed and latched before he left for work at night, but this time he had to rush out and forgot our bedroom window was still open. I went to bed with Boz lying beside me on the floor; sleep did not come easily to me, but just as I was beginning to relax and fall asleep suddenly there was this commotion of screeching, howling and Boz barking and growling that had me shooting out of bed, running about the bedroom shaking in fright, half asleep, trying to grab anything to use as a weapon, in case I needed to defend us. By now Boz had pushed the window open, wide enough for him to jump out into our front garden and there was so much more screeching and barking outside that it was a miracle James did not wake up. My neighbour came out and knocked on our door to ask what was happening, but I had no clue, as yet. I grabbed the dog by his collar so he could not run off into the darkness. Then we both saw a huge ginger cat slink off across the lawns with Boz madly straining against my firm grip. Boz wanted to chase the cat so desperately and would have run to anywhere if I let him go! I think the cat tried to climb through our bedroom window and the dog did exactly what he is trained to do, defend! Next day, I heard from most of the neighbourhood who had heard all the noise and excitement, but all were glad we were safe and seemed to know the 'cat burglar' well. Not his first night call in this neighbourhood!

After all this excitement any sleep was to elude me. However, God (unbeknown to me as yet) was after all these years whispering again, prompting and nudging me this time to open my drawer and read Jenna's book. The book seemed to quiver in my hands as I nervously started to read. It was a slim book with short chapters of different testimonies from all kinds of people who had experienced God answering prayers in incredible, even miraculous ways. One young woman had been born with a defect to her reproductive organs and yet after prayer had conceived against all medical odds. This testimony had me going back to read and reread it many times as it almost fit my experiences although I had had one normal pregnancy. Was it possible that God, still so distant, could answer my longing for another baby? Wasn't this selfish with all the pain in the world, surely God has bigger things in our world to consider than me and my desires?

Each time I thought this way, the whisper became stronger and more urgent until I fell into a deep sleep. I awoke with a renewed sense in my heart that I was much loved and dare I say in God's hands. I got up to waken James for school and found I was smiling and that this alien feeling wrapped around my heart was hope. Gordon came home from a long tiring night shift to a very different wife from the usual one. Later he was to tell me he could see something had changed inside me for the better. He could see light within; I had hope back! He went to bed after hearing of our night's adventures with Boz and the cat. No, I did not share a word about the book, this I nursed close for now. How can you explain something to another person when you don't understand any of it for yourself?

After Boz and I walked James to the village school, we continued through the fields and along the country lanes covering miles that sunny morning. As I walked, I sang and laughed and when we came to a bench I sat and for the very first time in my life I started to pray. The words were silent but heartfelt and I stumbled along not knowing if this was truly prayer or my inept fumbling with words but I sensed God graciously did not mind. St Augustine closely echoes my heart at this time, with his short prayer written in the 4th Century:

'Father I am seeking; I am hesitant and uncertain, but will You, O God, watch over every step of mine and guide me.'

Once we began to head for home, I thought this had to be madness, talking to an entity I wasn't sure existed and could not see or touch, yet I knew I could not stop myself; for the first time in years, life felt good, hope abounded and I sensed healing beginning in my soul. I remember bending over to give Boz a big hug, giggling happily as I thought of the night's events that led to my reading this awesome little book with such a powerful message. Even Boz had played his part in our family life drama. When next I met with Jenna, I gave her a big hug and thanked her over and over for lending me her little book which had succeeded in breaking me free of the bonds of grief and sorrow and set me on a healing path. She gently took my hands and earnestly said how it was important that I got to know God and His Son Jesus that what God desired most from all of us was a living relationship. He doesn't just want to hear our needs but wants all of us. Hearing her words, something in me grasped the urgency and I held fast to this mesmerizing concept of having a relationship with God. I never told her or anyone at that time, about the experiences I had as a child and the words the minister had spoken to me when I visited the Nairobi Cathedral. I kept silent, but God's whispers continued to encourage me and heal me. I certainly had travelled through some dark times but now I sensed with awe and wonder that just as the minister in Nairobi cathedral had told me, I was never alone, for God was there with me.

My praying continued daily, and as Christmas approached I took James to the Saxon village church for the first time. It was the Sunday before Christmas, and the annual Nativity and Carol service so the small stone building was packed. I had not been in a church building since our wedding in Hounslow and that one had been built in this century. This old church was so old and smelled of the centuries of candle wax and dust, maybe some mildew but also an encompassing sense of the sacred, of centuries of prayer and worship living in the very air we breathed. It was all welcoming and noisy as families hunted for seats. It was to be a lovely, joyful service and I enjoyed singing Christmas carols for the first time in a church and watching the children act out the ancient scenes of the nativity. As we walked home, I felt light and joyful and thoughtful as I went over the nativity in my head. Memories of Aileen's mother's words about

Jesus the Son of God came back to me and I determined then to learn and understand more about scripture and the God who found me. I would buy my first bible as a Christmas gift to myself. Christmas was a busy time for me as Gordon's mother; my father, sister and her new husband were coming for the traditional turkey dinner. Unfortunately, I felt ill all through Christmas and very tired my heart just not in the festivities. Gordon was adamant I took on too much and urged me to see our doctor in the New Year. To keep him happy I went, in early January and explained my symptoms. To my surprise he did a gentle internal examination, helped me sit up and arrange my clothing decently, then with a huge smile on his face, told me I was about 5 months pregnant! Together we laughed, as you do when you hear impossible good news. How can this be I asked? 'It is a Christmas miracle Kathleen, accept it and take care of the two of you', said my ecstatic doctor. I could not wait to share the wonderful, amazing news with Gordon and we hugged each other in disbelief and wonder. This was the time to tell him about my prayers, but something held me back. Gordon's mother came to help me so I could rest more than usual with a busy little son and ebullient, energetic dog. I was in such a state of euphoric joy and happiness having had my prayers answered, I stopped praying after all I had what I had asked for! How foolish we humans are and how we misunderstand the Almighty God, for He is not our puppet or our genie of the lamp, to do our will and grant our every wish and then step back out of sight until we have need of Him again. I was about to learn a very hard, important lesson in my first stages of building a relationship with my Creator. He sets importance in us being faithful and thankful in the good and bad days; never taking Him for granted is high on God's requirements, communicating with him day by day and not just when we want something from Him, but I did not know this; I would though soon!

Although I rested and did very little exertion, one evening I began the all too familiar pains of early labour and all the symptoms that go along with such a disaster. Thankfully Gordon and his mother were home and our doctor was so kind, but nature took its course and I miscarried. This time it was far worse as I was in the second trimester of pregnancy and the physical and emotional pain threatened to undo me. Yet something was different this time. I prayed an angry prayer berating God for what I saw as being cheated but quickly sensed my anger was very ill founded. As I awoke the following morning I had a new focus, a new understanding which seemed to come directly from God not from my own mind or thoughts. It seemed harsh yet I received it as a loving rebuke and knew I deserved it. It made perfect sense! How could I pray for the gift of a new child and then having received the promise turn my back and ignore the loving God who blessed me. I had taken my newfound joy as if I owned and deserved this prize and had stopped praying or even thinking of God. We cannot treat Almighty God like that and expect to get away with it.

Later I was to see the truth written out in the Holy scriptures as in Psalm 103 verse 11: "for as high as the heavens are above the earth, so great is His love for those who <u>fear Him.</u>" NIV.

This terrible, tragic loss taught me a much needed, if painful lesson, our Almighty God deserves and requires that we fear Him, that we live in awe and wonder and reverence of Him always, not play Him fast and loose. I sincerely asked for His forgiveness and received a deep sense of peace, that all would be well. Some readers may ask does God really do such things? My only response to such a question is this; my biological father would physically punish me when I broke a promise, lied or was discovered to have behaved in some flagrantly disrespectful way that defied parental rules. I hated being punished in this way, it humiliated me, more than it hurt, yet I knew I had let him down badly by disappointing him. I can understand that my heavenly Father would also set the standard high for how I was to behave and there would be dire consequences when I transgressed.

Revelation 3 verse 19 reminds us all "those whom I love I rebuke and discipline. So be earnest and repent."

This incredible event strengthened my tenuous relationship and I had a fresh understanding of trust. Would there ever be an end to the lessons I badly needed to learn to live this spiritual relationship? Forty-one years on, I know the answer is no, the learning is day by day, and lifelong.

The proof of His faithfulness always comes and four months later I was to have confirmed by my doctor that I was again pregnant and this time I made sure God was centre in my heart and not an afterthought. I praised and thanked God daily for His wonderful grace in all things, not only those I sought. This pregnancy was normal and uneventful apart from continuous nausea, which seemed well worth the joy. During this time of waiting, we fostered a young boy, Simon, who went to school with James. He lived along the road from us. His parents were going through a difficult time and Social Services approved us to short term foster Simon. It was a delight to have two boys who were also great friends and we enjoyed many family outings together. My pregnancy progressed smoothly despite the ongoing nausea. We agreed on needing to move to a larger house with more than two bedrooms, so had our bungalow up for sale. The house sold quickly and Simon's mother came to take him home, all wonderful timing before we moved to our new home and our second baby was born. We were ready to take our leave of Oxfordshire, as Gordon had a very long daily commute to London Heathrow Airport where he worked.

On the day of the move, even our house-movers could have been picked by angels, as they refused to let me (heavily pregnant) lift a finger and always made sure there was a chair for me to rest upon. They insisted on cleaning up before we left our old house and made the whole enterprise such a delight. Our new home was in Buckinghamshire and had three large bedrooms and a very tiny garden but was within metres walking distance of the elementary school. Many families lived around us and I looked forward to making new friends.

James hated change and it took him many months to settle especially having to start a new school. Poor boy was to have too many changes one after another. Within a couple of months of moving I was in hospital having our 'miracle' baby son, Jonah. I was very scared going into labour, praying nothing would be wrong with the baby, and all would be straightforward. He took about 36 hours to enter the world, and I was very glad of the epidural injection to assist with the pain. At 7pm on January 14th, Jonah slid into the world after one almighty push and he seemed so tiny, only 5 pounds 6 ounces, so perfect in every detail. Gordon was allowed to remain with me for the birth, (no such privileges when James was born as fathers were firmly closed out from the delivery room). He was ecstatic for both of us as I was exhausted! We cried with joy as we gazed on our perfect second son, not daring to think how this should not have happened. How did it happen? Gordon had no such existential thoughts, but I knew emphatically this child was a gift from God. Tangible evidence from Him 'who whispers His presence to me'! Once I was back in the ward, tucked up in bed, so ready for a good sleep, I prayed with heartfelt rejoicing and gratitude that flowed up from my depths like rivers; my tears of joy provided the water! Silently I spoke these words of a commitment I did not fully understand back then as I do today; nonetheless every word was heart felt and a true promise:

> *'My heavenly Father, I cannot find the words to thank you for our second precious little son, nothing I can ever do will repay this gift, but I do promise to study your bible and learn all I can about you God and Your Son Jesus. Thank you for making Yourself known to me when I was only a child and for never letting me out of Your sight. Thank you for bothering with me who has so little to offer but Lord, I promise to give my life to You from this time forward. I will serve You and Your Son in any way You ask and will never forsake You. Amen'*

With these words echoing through me I fell into a deep sleep. Some hours later, I had the most hideous dream, really a nightmare, the details of which remain with me today forty-one years later as clearly as that night. In years to come when I shared the details with my Spiritual Advisor, he suggested my early intrigue and interest into things of the shadows and darkness were angry at my commitment made to God and tried to harm me. You who read this will have your own thoughts but

I agree with John, this was a spiritual attack, possibly upon my life but at least meant to scare and disable me.

In the dream, I know I am in my hospital bed and that Jonah is in the nursery in his little bassinet. I have just finished the above prayer to God when three menacing, tall, black figures stoop over my bed and try to pick me up and pull me away ... I struggle, screaming when brilliant light breaks all over the bed and the figures seem to melt away as I wake up screaming the words "I do not belong to you, I belong to Jesus".

The woman sharing the hospital room with me was shaking me awake and said the noise I was making was like an animal dying in a trap. She said I sounded as if I was fighting for my life! Maybe I had been? Nurses came running and helped me quieten down and one stayed with me until I fell asleep again. Thankfully, no more dreaming I never again want one like that. The things of darkness are opposed to God and to His Son, the Light of the world and will try anything to deter us from committing our life to serving our heavenly Father, Almighty God. I think this nightmare was a glimpse at the spiritual power encounter trying to prevent me from making my commitment to Christ Jesus. But now I belonged to Him in every way, having made my commitment of faith and I had been baptized as a small baby so now my spiritual growth began in earnest.

God took away all fear of that event but left me the clear details so I can never forget that the devil creeps around like a lion seeking any he can destroy. I also learned to love and trust this scripture written by St Paul in his letter to the Romans chapter 8, titled "More Than Conquerors": verses 37 to 39, NIV.

> *"No, in all these things we are more than conquerors through him who loved us. For I am convinced that neither death nor life, neither angels nor demons, neither the present nor the future, nor any powers, neither height nor depth, nor anything else in all creation, will be able to separate us from the love of God in Christ Jesus, our Lord."*

God had given new life that night and only He could take it away, nothing and nobody has the power to destroy life. The destructive power of death was destroyed when Jesus died on the cross at Calvary. I had survived my first, but it was not to be the last power encounter between God and His enemy who hated to see anyone rejoice over God's grace. I survived not through any power or privilege I held, but utterly and completely through God alone. Years on, I know how important it is to place ourselves under God's protection, on a daily basis. This is the reason, St Paul wrote in his letter to the Ephesians Chapter 6 about the need to put on the full armour of God so we can remain strong in the Lord and His mighty power when the enemy comes against us. Sometimes we try to live ahead of God's will for us, we get out of step and then fall into the enemy's traps that are strategically placed to take us by surprise and cause us the maximum fear and anxiety. I have learned this by painful experience and still find myself stumbling from time to time. I am getting better at recognizing what is happening and placing myself firmly back in God's hands.

Chapter 5

"For you know that we dealt with each of you as a father deals with his own children, encouraging, comforting and urging you to live lives worthy of God, who calls you into His kingdom and glory"

-1 Thessalonians 2: verse 11.NIV

Bringing our new baby boy home was a very happy, long anticipated occasion, but soon challenges made themselves felt.

James having had us to himself for nine years, resented giving up his 'only child status'. Almost overnight his behaviour became difficult and if he could make his little brother cry he did. I understood about the sibling rivalry and tried to be empathetic for James' unhappiness at having to share us. When we could, we spent time as a family as much as one can with a newborn in the home, trying to help James adjust to having a baby brother.

James did not want to leave me, which meant he didn't want to go to school or play with his friends. It was a hard time for him and I was trying to learn how to balance the age difference between the boys and not doing a very good job it seems. My father did not help matters when he would just turn up and expect to stay for weeks sharing James' bedroom yet taking it over as his own. We only had three bedrooms, so the biggest was given to James with room for two beds plus other furniture and doubled as his playroom. Hindsight is always wonderful; we should have moved the baby into our room but at that time with Gordon a shift worker, coming home early mornings or very late, the baby needed to be in a quiet room, so he had the smallest bedroom. James must have felt he was losing all his fixed points of security and nobody cared. This was not true, for we did care but unsure how to change things for the better. We could see he was suffering. Grandfather bossed and nagged poor James over every little thing and life got very stressful for me, as I edged between them. More than once I lost my temper and yelled at my father, to leave James alone and if anyone was to discipline him it would be Gordon or me. There was much tension in the air and it made all of us miserable.

We all breathed with relief when Dad suddenly left for who knows where until his next visit. We loved him and made allowances for his grief and loneliness but having him stay was a huge strain at times.

Meanwhile, my heart was reminding me of my promise to God made in the hospital on the night Jonah was born. The year of his birth was one of the hottest on record (1976) and I would walk a lot with the baby in the pram, the dog on his leash, and James sometimes came too grumbling and dragging his feet. Sometimes all of us, including the pram wheels, would get tangled up in the leash and we must have looked so odd to people we passed. Our dog Boz was gentle and loving yet so disobedient; he just wanted to run free. One hot afternoon we took another avenue to the village centre with promises of ice cream for James if he walked nicely! This new way brought us to the Anglican Church called "All Saints". I slowed down as we passed by taking it all in; the modern red brick exterior surrounded by a small beautifully kept garden. It had welcoming, warm appeal and I took note of the times of Sunday worship. When I told Gordon I was going to church that Sunday, he scoffed at me and refused to come along. Undeterred, I walked to church and found a warm welcome from many of the congregation although the rector was rather an odd fellow but seemed very kind. Slowly I became used to the Anglican format of services and especially enjoyed those that carried a reminder of my African church visits!

One Sunday, as I was leaving and shaking Reverend Eric's hand at the door, I found myself asking him about me and Confirmation and having Jonah baptized. He promised to call on me during the week to discuss both events.

James had been baptized in the church close to the family home in Cheltenham where my mother's funeral took place and she is buried. Since her death, the house had been sold and my father succumbed to his itinerant travels.

I asked Gordon if he was agreeable to this baptism being planned at 'All Saints' and he nodded but said nothing more. This was to remain his usual stance on church going ... more of a 'as long as you do not expect me to participate sort of nod'! Especially when I told him that Reverend Eric would be coming to our home each week to prepare me for Confirmation. I was excited to have an opportunity to learn more as my ignorance of 'church practice' was embarrassingly high. I really enjoyed our church services and was becoming familiar with sacramental terms, liturgical practises and the Gospel stories, but always had many questions for Reverend Eric. He was quite odd and was given to say from the pulpit no less, that we (the congregation) were all stupid compared to him for he was a learned theologian! It amazed me that despite these insults, people loved him. I came in for plenty of the intellectual criticism as I continuously asked my basic and to him stupid questions. He had this habit of loudly sucking in his breath and fiercely rubbing his hands together, looking as though he was gearing up for the debate of the century! Regrettably, I was never any good at his standard of theological debate. Some 40 years on, I now recognize how much theology he really did know and appreciate how much he taught me. Reverend Eric's memory wasn't too good, so we were warned to keep reminding him of the date of Jonah's baptism, because he often forgot, and was also known to forget the baby's name and make something up. He was quirky and eccentric but a generous, kindly soul who brought both myself and later Gordon and my father to a deep faith in Jesus Christ. Sadly, Eric could not take the baptism after all our plans, being away with the Bishop that weekend, so we made do with the Curate whose very broad Irish brogue was almost impossible to understand. Once the service was over, he never said another word during the reception but steadily ate everything in sight! He was a bachelor after all!

Life continued and I enjoyed my beautiful family both in the home and my newer family in the church. James still did not fully accept his brother, which made for some tense moments but both boys were so dear to us and we wanted to help them both as best we could. I loved my new friends and began to help teach in Sunday School after my confirmation, but Gordon was still very distant about matters of faith in Christ. On the evening of my Confirmation service, held in another town because of the large group, Gordon became unusually critical and hurtful.

Later, he was to ask me for forgiveness for his words, spoken because he felt threatened by this other Being in my life. I guess I spoke too much about my faith and my love for Jesus as any new Christian does and Gordon was fed up hearing it all the time. There would come a time when he went through this himself and he found how difficult it is to keep quiet about the Good News of Christ. However, this was not for a few more years! During the interim he occasionally came to Family services, which helped me as James could be very restless in church. One evening at work, speaking to his Best Man, Harry, all about my confirmation and my tiresome habit of trying to coerce him to attend church, he was staggered to have Harry gently encourage him to find out more about Christianity. Harry and his wife had become very involved in their Baptist Church and although we did not know this, they were praying for Gordon to find his way into a faith in Christ. Gordon had been challenged and the effects of our friends' prayers began to make themselves felt. I noticed a softening in his attitude and a new willingness to join me on a Sunday. As he was slowly awakening to the touch of God, the enemy came prowling by and we were beset with financial worries and severe health problems, often knocked down but never beaten. Our Lord Jesus picked us up time and again and led us through the adversity. Jonah developed severe asthma and had many stays in the hospital pediatric ward, often in an oxygen tent. Back in the 1970s little medication was available for asthma. Thankfully the medical care he was given pulled him through although he still suffers with it today at 41. These times were terrifying as he was so young and vulnerable. James suffered serious croup as a very young boy but grew out of it by the time he started school.

It finally dawned on me how much misery oozed out of the atmosphere in this house. There were times when I would wake in the night and our room seemed to be immersed in a thick, impenetrable darkness. I spoke to Reverend Eric about this and he suggested I pray the Lord's Prayer which I did every time, it helped and slowly the darkness went away. It was such a strange time. I felt there was an unseen battle being waged around us, later I came to know there was. Some years later I understood how all around us in the unseen dimension, the evil spirits battle with those who seek to live by God's Spirit. St Paul teaches about this very truth in his letter to the Ephesians Chapter 6 in the New Testament. I urge you to read this for yourselves as it is so important for our protection; it begins at verse 12: *'for our struggle is not against flesh and blood, but against the powers of this dark world .... and against the spiritual forces of evil in the heavenly realms.'* **NIV**

Since our move, the house never seemed warm or a place which had ever been filled with joy and love. Often, we spoke of wishing we had never bought the house and began to look for a move somewhere else. Later, we found out the previous owners had lots of sadness and trials in the time they lived in this house. This dismal sense continued. One afternoon James slipped and as he fell, he tried to stop himself, but momentum caused his hand to hit against the weakened porch door glass window, his hand broke the glass cutting his hand very severely. As I rushed to find the cause of his loud cry, I saw blood gushing from the many deep cuts. Quickly, I rushed him and the baby into the car, his arm wrapped in several clean tea towels, to the nearest Emergency Room, whereupon he endured over thirty sutures in his hand. He was such a stoic boy and never cried during the painful procedure. Bad things kept happening, but there was always an unseen angel close by to prevent complete disaster. The ER doctor who cared for James could not understand how nerve damage had been avoided and also how fortunate he was not to slice into his artery close by in his wrist. Soon after this, I began to sense body changes and knew I was pregnant again. I said nothing but privately prayed for a daughter this time. Within a couple of weeks, I began to experience a fierce pain in my shoulder and unpleasant sensations in my abdomen area. I developed a fever and felt very ill. Gordon called out the family doctor who diagnosed stomach flu and blamed the shoulder pain on Boz always tugging me when he was his leash! No better after a few days, I went to our medical clinic and saw another doctor, this visit turned out to be very fortuitous as he immediately put together the fierce shoulder pain and other symptoms diagnosing an ectopic pregnancy and I was admitted to hospital for urgent surgery within the hour. The gynaecologist agreed with the diagnosis and also spent some time reviewing my history with all my pregnancies. His conclusion was strong advice that as I had to have surgery to remove the ectopic pregnancy, I should also have tubal ligation to prevent more dangerous pregnancies arising. Gordon and I both agreed this was sensible and I gave my consent. I had the surgery early in the evening as they could not wait any longer or my fallopian tube could burst. Later I was told that I was very hard to rouse after the anaesthetic and kept falling back into a deep slumber. The next day the Recovery Room RN came to see me on the ward to find out if I was truly alright as she told me my vital signs showed I was in grave danger for a time and she was very concerned that I would die. Since I was only thirty-one and had a young baby of eighteen months and an older son, she told me she prayed for me to make a full recovery. I thanked God for her prayer. What I remembered of this event was very different. I seemed to hear or perhaps feel the nurse shaking me awake and calling my name over and over and then I was aware that 'I' was looking down on this scene. 'I' seemed to be up close to the ceiling of the Recovery Room and could see curtains closed around my bed and leads connected to my body, also an intravenous drip which was attached to my arm, as my body lay in the bed. The body in the bed was shivering and the nurses were wrapping a foil blanket around her to warm her body temperature and then suddenly a doctor appeared and placed an oxygen mask on her face, looking very concerned. Just as I was aware of the scene beneath me it changed and a voice said into my awareness 'this is not your time, I am sending you back!" There was a rushing sound and then 'I' was in my body and an external voice said, "her eyes are opening." Then I slipped into a normal sleep state. When I awoke properly, I was back in my ward with a nurse washing my face and hands. I felt my body for the foil blanket and asked her why I had needed it. She gave me a very strange look and asked me how I could possibly have known that, as I was slipping into a coma at the time that occurred. I shared with her what I could remember of my odd experience of being up at ceiling level, looking down on my body, and the activity around my bed. "Just put it down to an 'out of body experience'" she said as though this explained everything! What I kept to myself was hearing the voice telling me this was not my time. I knew the voice, recognizing it instinctively, as my Father in heaven and stored this new mystery in my heart. This whole experience changed me, physically of course due to the nature of the surgery; emotionally, because now I had personal proof that I belonged to God in Christ and He watched over me; spiritually because my faith and trust was strengthening and developing in new ways. I felt less fearful and anxious as now I knew all our moments, all our tomorrows are in His loving hands and control. Time belongs to God not to mankind. He and he alone ordain the time of our birth and our death and we are helpless to divert or overt the passage of time. This releases us from a huge burden of guesswork and striving to discern the 'right time' for things in our life. If we allow our God to guide us then His Time will always be followed perfectly. I learned more of this during my hospital stay. Because of the scare I had given everyone, to keep an eye on me after my surgery, the staff moved me into a Critical Care section. Looking back, I discern I was really moved because God was preparing in advance for a spiritual need which would unfold that day. A young South African mother was brought in by ambulance, hemorrhaging badly after she miscarried. She was in very bad shape and as they worked on her, her poor husband was left alone to wander about with tears rolling down his cheeks and fear etched on his face. Michael looked so vulnerable and afraid that my heart went out to him and I called him over to my bed and suggested he sat in the chair beside my bed. We began to talk about our beloved South Africa and what brought each of us to England. I told him about Gordon and our family and my struggles to have our second child. He and his wife had one son, Anthony, and dearly wanted another. As midnight came and went, I found myself telling him my experiences of God as a young child in Nairobi and the wonderful gifts more recently. For the first time in my life, I invited Michael, this stranger who had become a fellow pilgrim during the night to prayer with me for his wife to fully recover and for her to be blessed with a successful pregnancy in the Lord's time. It felt so right and yet so odd to pray like this as he told me he and his family were Orthodox Jews, yet this did not matter as we believed in the same God and knew He was present in that place. As we opened our eyes, we saw the doctor looking around for Michael with great news of his wife; all was well and she would be able to try for another pregnancy in a few months. In the remaining days of our hospital stay, Gordon met Michael and he and his wife became firm friends with us that lasted many years until they left for Australia. They would invite us to join them for their Friday prayers and supper which was a wonderful experience. She was more extrovert about her life and their faith, and amazed that her quiet, shy husband had prayed with me. We all agreed that this was a God inspired meeting at the hospital, in His time! To our God there are no boundaries between different expressions of faith, only opportunities for new bonds of love. This was a beautiful time for both families and we have never forgotten them and uphold them to the Lord. From each other we learn so much more about the many characteristics of our mighty God and how we shared so much as Christians and Jews. Back home once again from hospital, brought the overshadowing gloom and presence of shadowy negativity casting its cloud over us. Gordon and I seriously began house hunting, but this house of ours did not want to let us go. No one wanted to purchase it from us. Many people came but sensed it was not warm and welcoming and would make a muttered apology of it not being what they wanted as they swiftly left. We became desperate, until I remembered that my Jesus promised that whatever we asked of him, he would provide. Once again, I began my prayer quest but this time with more understanding and with a strong sense of worship, respect and humility. His answer was not long in coming via a neighbour who told us about the builder of a small development of new builds on land about 5-minute walk, from our present house, who might consider taking our house in exchange for a new build. Gordon quickly set up a meeting with the builder who came and valued our house and made his offer of an exchange. He had built a small number of four bedroomed homes with garages and larger gardens than we had, so we would gain another bedroom, larger yard and could save money by fitting out the kitchen ourselves. It seemed a very comfortable deal and it all went through very effortlessly. We soon moved into our spacious new home where the boys had their own bedrooms, even with one for grandfather when he turned up. We all felt happy about the move and I asked Reverend Eric to come and pray as we dedicated this blessing to the Lord. I noticed the negative cloud had disappeared and we began to really enjoy life to the full. We invited my father to live with us permanently, after he was diagnosed with cancer and at his suggestion I began to work fulltime again as he was home for the boys after school. I was offered a job in Flight Operations for McAlpine Helicopters and began to truly appreciate the opportunity to earn money and extend my experiences outside of the home, once again. It had been a long time and I had to rediscover my confidence and how to use my brain again. My father's health was stable with medication for many years and it was invaluable having him care for the boys whilst we worked. Dad slowly developed newfound patience and grew to have strong relationships with both his grandsons.

Our church life was developing too. Gordon would attend more and more with me and the boys enjoyed Sunday School, which I also led. Our faith grew and so did our happiness and sense of wellbeing. It was on a Good Friday that Gordon first truly heard the whisper from God, calling him to Christ. Something in the sermon that particular day broke the residual coldness in his heart and he found he was weeping uncontrollably until he was felt utterly cleansed. He found this all so strange and rather overwhelming yet joyful and hopeful, but it wasn't too long before he was trying to analyse what had happened and dissect the whole experience. He was clearly sitting on the fence and not ready to make any commitment to following Christ and I feared he would slip back to his old agnostic position. I began to gently nudge him towards making a commitment, suggesting he needed to get off the uncomfortable fence and make a choice for or against but have the courage of his convictions at the very least.

One evening Dad was out and the boys asleep so we had the sitting room to ourselves. Gordon asked me how he should proceed in making his profession of faith in Christ. Talk about the blind leading the blind! I remembered a book I read that had the Sinner's Prayer in it; so I found this and asked Gordon to say it out loud and then I prayed asking our Father, to take Gordon into his heart and show him the love he had for this prodigal son. Neither of us was prepared for what happened next, this was so unlike my gentle slow process of growing in faith. One minute Gordon was talking and smiling and the next he was there in body but clearly his attention and mind was elsewhere and remained so for over an hour. His face glowed with radiance all the while with his hands upraised and his lips moving silently as some beatific conversation continued between him and the Lord. After that experience my husband was never the same man again. Over that sacred hour he had entered into a covenant with God and was forever changed, transformed is closer to the truth. Gordon had submitted his life to his Creator God, body, mind and spirit and God had gifted him with the outpouring of his Holy Spirit, empowering him to protect and guide his family under God. I felt so privileged to witness this amazing transformation and probably would not have believed it possible if I had not been present. I have to confess that I felt somewhat envious as my coming to Christ seemed so tame and long winded compared to Gordon. Christ had to help me let go of my envy and just rejoice my husband was home!

This change made some things difficult for Gordon as he had to learn the art of spiritual discernment and sensitivity. He wanted to evangelize everyone who crossed his path and many were not yet ready for the Good News of Christ and some expressed this very rudely and hurtfully.

Gordon became a wonderful man of God and learned quickly from the Bible, showing his true worth as a man of wisdom and strength. He became Reverend Eric's right hand man for many years as he served the church as Parish Warden.

Our home became a haven for Bible study groups and the Youth group which caused my poor agnostic father to hide away in his bedroom! If Reverend Eric appeared at our house Dad disappeared quickly but he never said anything to us about our growing faith in Christ. As my father's cancer became more aggressive, he clearly was taking note of our belief in God. One evening he said how he found our Christian friends so kind and loyal; they all loved Dad and made time to talk to him. Some months on as I helped him into bed, he held hold of my hand and said he was sorry to be such a disappointment to me when I was so kind to him. What do you mean I asked him, well he replied, I know how much you want me to believe in your Jesus and I only wish I could? I asked him what was stopping him. How could Jesus possibly forgive someone as faithless as me he asked, eyes glistening. I was so choked I could not answer him but squeezed his hand and as I said good night, I mumbled Jesus loves us all the same. Telling Gordon afterwards about this conversation I felt badly at not taking it further with Dad. Had I missed an amazing opportunity? God's time came perfectly not too many days later. I received a booklet from Burrswood Christian Healing Centre in Sussex, England each month as I supported their ministry. As I read the newest booklet, I noticed the times of their weekly service open to everyone and felt a strong spiritually jolt. Turning to Gordon, I told him that I felt I had to drive my father to this Healing service as soon as possible. As I spoke the words, I felt anxiety that my father would refuse my invitation but next morning I made it anyway. To my utter amazement, Dad said yes that sounds good!

We left early on the morning of the Healing service and it was a long drive of over 3 hours to get to Burrswood, but we had plenty of time or so I thought. Still new to all this following God's Spirit, I had not prayed for protection for our journey, thus I had left us open for the enemy to use tactics to send me round in circles as we approached our destination trying to make me give up in frustration perhaps or to make us so late, we missed the service! To my amazement it was my father who asked quietly maybe you should pray and so I did. We soon were driving down the long approach avenue to the Centre and arrived just in time for the beginning of the service. It was held in their ancient stone church built in the days of grand estates and clearly was very popular. The service was short and very simple; soon the invitation was made for those who had come for the laying on of hands to come forward and kneel before the altar of God and ask God for the healing they needed. Oops, I thought Dad is not going to want to go up for any public anointing but to my utter amazement he was one of the first up on his feet and moving forward to kneel before the Holy altar. This sight moved me to tears. Quietly I sat in my pew praying for God's will to be released for everyone in this place. There was a holy hush enveloping us, nobody made a sound it seemed even the stones laid in the floor and walls held their breath. After a long sacred silence that felt so natural, the organ gave a note and a beautiful voice began to sing out a simple praise to God. This marked the end of the service but not many people moved.

After the service Dad remained in his seat very quiet and reflective so I moved away to give him space. When I looked back some while later, he was being led to another room by the priest who led the service.

This whole time felt ordained by God, this was truly a holy appointment and I was so thankful we had come. Whilst I waited for Dad I had tea with some of the other visitors and learned more of the Healing ministry of Burrswood. After at least two hours Dad appeared looking relaxed, joyful and all the usual stress of pain removed from his face. He looked so much younger and yet tired as if he had completed some very vital tasks. I so wished he had his healing! On the long, journey home he was very quiet, so I did not ask any questions although I was bursting to know what he and the minister had discussed. As we came to a stop before our garage at home, I asked him if he was glad that we had gone to Burrswood that day. He took his time answering, I almost thought he wasn't going to say anything at all, but then he quietly spoke. My father had received prayer and made his own peace with the God and Father he had fought against recognizing all his life and then he uttered these words 'I am healed now'. As these words left his lips, I knew with a certainty, as though it was all laid out before me, the manner of his healing was spiritual not physical, and I knew that he understood as I did the implications. I held tight to his hand and then we walked towards the house in tacit agreement that all this was to remain between ourselves. Not many days passed when Dad asked me to invite Reverend Eric to the house as he wanted to speak with him. I never knew what passed between them on that visit, but it was emotionally charged for both of them. I could tell it was momentous as Dad had such an aura of peace. Some days later, one evening he told Gordon and me that he had made his commitment to Jesus Christ and now could face his Creator when his time came to go home. The weeks passed with the usual business of family life, yet Dad was a transformed man, it was as if all his military harshness and emotional distance had left him and we all enjoyed the novel experience of the gentle, peace of a man living in step with his heavenly Father. It was about 3 months after our Burrswood visit that Dad went into hospital no longer able to stay at home as the cancer was now everywhere, including his brain and he slipped in and out of a coma most of the time. Some visits he was lucid for a short time and I would pray and he would smile; I treasure the memory of these all too brief times. I would sit beside him in his private room and wonder at the long journey and the life time of needless pain he had borne as he slowly edged his way towards redemption and new life in Christ. Why do some of us take so long to come back to our origins as a child of God? It makes me weep to think of the needless suffering we go through as we refuse to recognize our heavenly Father. My Dad had been a wonderful father, strict yes but always scrupulously fair and so encouraging in motivating me to believe in myself. He was not evil or bad, he could be impatient and never suffered fools lightly; he had served in many wars as a courageous obedient soldier defending his country and his people; like so many soldiers he had his scars and used alcohol for a while to keep the bad memories away until us his family helped him believe in goodness and innocence again. My father and I were both children of Africa and shared a deep love and respect for all who claim this for themselves. He enabled me to find out for myself my own strengths and weaknesses and taught me to laugh at myself, to have courage and take the chances to experience the excitement of adventure and to never allow anyone to bully or threaten me. I owe him so much and will always respect him as I remember him with love and gratitude. Why does humankind allow pride, or maybe it is fear of being judged that keeps us from approaching the only One who already and always has known us and sees us as we truly are; why do people like my father hide away refusing to acknowledge the Being who gave them life when they could have known such comfort and joy all their days. I was so thankful that at least he would face the eternal Judge having made his peace with God at long last. Dad's passing was so different to that of my mother, this time I felt grief and sadness of course but such joy too because he had his healing in such a wonderful lasting way and I know we shall meet up again one day. Our church friends all rejoiced with us having witnessed Dad before and after his encounter with His Lord and Saviour Jesus Christ. Dad's funeral service was such a celebration of his new life; the church was full and the mood victorious. Reverend Eric preached a very moving sermon for he too had been touched by this experience. Gordon read the moving passage from 1 Peter 1:

> *"Now you have purified yourselves by obeying the truth so that you have sincere love for one another deeply, from the heart. For you have been born again, not of perishable seed, but of imperishable, through the living and enduring word of God, For, all people are like grass and all their glory is like the flowers of the fields; the grass withers and*

the flowers fall, but the word of God endures forever."1 Peter 1: 22 ff NIV

Chapter 6

"Blessed is the one whose sin the Lord does not count against them and in whose spirit is no deceit. When I kept silent, my bones wasted away through my groaning all day long. I said, 'I will confess my transgressions to the Lord' and you forgave the guilt of my sin. You are my hiding place; you will protect me from trouble and with songs of deliverance."

-Psalm 32:verses3, 5b, 7.NIV

God hopefully looked at our family with some gladness; both Gordon and I had committed ourselves to following Christ and were part of His living church; seeking to serve in various ways. Yet from His perspective we clearly needed much refining; we had so much more to learn as we deepened our roots in Him. The next few years were to be looked back on as the years of refining, moulding and being set free from the tentacles of the enemy. Oh yes! The enemy still had a firm hold on parts of our lives. We just did not see it that way, although the effects made themselves known in different scenarios. All people following Jesus are not immune from adversity and we were still ignorant of the enemy's tactics and what to watch carefully so we did not stumble spiritually. I was to be brought almost to my grave by a deadly illness and Gordon would find this tested his faith like nothing else could. But for now, life went on. We all missed my father very much as he had been an integral part of the family for so long. I thought Jonah would suffer the most as he and my father were great buddies, but he bravely declared at hearing of his death that Granddad was now in heaven so we should all be happy, and not sad. Out of the mouths of babes comes the truth so often; we took our cue from Jonah and most of the time had joy, but sadness still crept into my heart and brought all its friends with it, anxiety, insecurity etc.!

We were now attending a Bible Group led by an American evangelist, Rod Anderson, who had a special gift for teaching from God's word. He brought the Bible alive for us and we learned so much under his unequivocal instruction. You either believed the entire Bible to be God's word of truth or you were not a Christian in his view, he permitted no dividing up the Bible into pieces one might reject or favour; it was all or nothing! He revealed the Old Testament to his audience like unwrapping a precious jewel, it was a marvelous course. The people we came to meet over the time of the study came from different church back grounds, but all were rooted in what they termed 'being born again of the Spirit of God' and exercising spiritual gifts in their service to God. This was all very new to us and we soaked up what we heard like sponges. Years on, we understand about receiving new spiritual information in a discerning manner, as not everything is always from God; the enemy will even try to sell a counterfeit Christian message to the gullible. It takes time to develop your own spiritual radar and we fell into many traps, but our faithful Jesus Christ was always close to help us out and sensitively lead us to the truth. One such example was being told that unless we spoke in a spiritual 'tongue' and fell over in 'the spirit' when prayed for, we were not filled with God's Spirit so therefore **not real Christians**! Again, it took years for us to learn the truth that those who called upon Jesus as their Saviour and Redeemer were gifted with the Holy Spirit and **_are real_**

**Christian**. We needlessly lived under a sense of condemnation and judgement that was very damaging. God does not make following Him through His Son difficult, or place pitfalls to disarm us, these come from the enemy. Simply put, God wants everyone to willingly follow Him through a relationship based upon giving and receiving unconditional love and all the rest flows from hereon. God has three characteristics: Father, Son and Holy Spirit; indivisible as one communion of truth, so if you believe in one characteristic you also believe in all three.

One young man with the Bible group always arrived alone and we tried to befriend him by inviting him home for dinner on many occasions. He and James got on well and he helped James in his spiritual growth for which we were very grateful, but he was an odd person, socially. All his conversation no matter what subject or topic included him quoting scripture verses. It felt like conversing with a concordance instead of a person. One visit, in frustration I asked him why he did this and clearly my question was taken as an insult for he never accepted another of our invites to supper. James still spent time with him, but I was clearly a grave disappointment to him, lacking heavily in my spiritual development! Over time I sensed and Gordon agreed that he was worshipping scripture instead of the Godhead, a form of idolatry perhaps? This was to be another warning lesson for us, never to allow ourselves to be enticed to veer away, from worshipping God himself. The way to the Godhead is a straight path with no deviations to worship any other entities, however spiritual. Scripture is given, to reveal and point us towards God in Christ and is never to be worshipped for its own sake.

During these years, Gordon and I were taking on more leadership roles in the Anglican Church we attended, with Reverend Eric's encouragement. I had been the Youth and Sunday School Leader for some time and we had a wonderful group of vibrant young people who loved coming round to chat and to study God's word. This gave me my first challenge in leadership. One evening two of our precious older youth who had recently set the date for their wedding, came to see us in a terrible state. Phil's brother (who was to be his best man at the wedding) had had a severe car accident was critically injured and his life was in jeopardy! The young couple begged us to pray for his healing. In my heart, I was full of trepidation as I had never done this before and felt so unworthy of the task, but placing all my faith in Christ, we joined hands and prayed in strength and faith for his healing and for him to be present at the wedding in a few weeks' time. This was to be the first time I experienced this phenomenon ... *as we prayed I had a picture in my mind, of the injured young man in his hospital bed surrounded by gently undulating blue radiance;* this I ' or rather sensed, was the Holy Spirit healing him, totally. So convinced was I that I shared this with the couple; confirming his brother would be beside him as best man at their wedding! On the happy day, the brother arrived on crutches but made it and stood beside Phil just as God had promised. This gave all of us a boost about trusting in God even when we felt weak and unworthy, for He does not fail us. This sense of healing when I see the blue undulating radiance has happened whilst I have prayed for others on some occasions, each time the ill person has been brought back from the brink of death. All the Lord our God's powerful work had absolutely nothing to do with me except my obedience in prayer.

At a meeting with Reverend Eric and our Bishop it was suggested that I should make a formal application to the Bishop to be considered for Lay Leadership training with a view to being licensed. This all went smoothly and it was not long before I handed over the Youth ministry to another person to allow me to meet the training criteria (I was also working full time). Gordon's shift work schedule helped a lot as he was often home during the day to keep an eye on the boys especially in school holidays. They were growing older and could be relied upon to behave most of the time!

The Diocese of Oxford had just initiated a Christian Training Scheme for mature students like me and so I attended classes twice a week in the evening and some weekends for four years to complete the training. I loved the course, it was a revelation as we enjoyed Old and New Testament studies; sermon preparation and preaching studies; prayer life studies; liturgical studies and many more. My favourite came towards the very end of the course for the final year we trained in Pastoral Clinical Studies. I found every class so interesting and could apply so much to my own life experiences. Our tutor told me privately I had an aptitude for this whole topic and she urged me to follow up by applying to the Marlow Pastoral Foundation. This Christian vocational training was over four years and would enable me to have a qualification for clinical and pastoral counselling. This sounded very exciting and another wonderful challenge, so I began as soon as I had my Lay Leader license to minister in our churches. I had become a lifelong student and loved it. Looking back God must have given me some extraordinary gift to endure all these training courses, work and be a full-time mother and wife. I rarely felt under pressure, rather I felt energized and loved the course curriculum. Now

God was surely part of the agenda, for without me ever realizing at the time, this was to be His way of ensuring my deep and much needed healing. A mandatory part of the course meant we all had to endure two years of personal therapy, meeting individually twice a month. If anyone had otherwise suggested I had therapy I would have been very insulted and resistant, but I and the others had no choice in the matter and to begin with we all just took it in our stride as part of the course content.

Around the same time, Gordon enrolled on a one-year pastoral healing course "Shepherding God's Flock"; this opened his eyes to God's healing path for his own wounds and scars held deep since he was a small boy. I love the way God's timing for everything is perfect! Here we were both united in our Christian walk of faith, embarking on healing journeys at the same time, yet taking different paths that made it so personal allowing us to be open and sensitive.

Out of my personal therapy came the surprise of release from the wounds caused when I was sexually assaulted as a nine-year-old. It was the one and only session I had with a male therapist and something about his gentle Godly spirit loosened my shame and humiliation so that the deeply held "secret' burst out in the open and it felt so right to talk about the terrible events, of so long ago. At the end of my session, I felt purified and healed for the first time in over 20 years and fully realized that I had nothing to be shameful or humiliated about, the cause of everything was the responsibility of my sick, perverted relative. I understood now how keeping this 'secret' had spoiled my relationship with Gordon and when I arrived home, I shared everything with him for the first time. I was still anxious that Gordon would in some way consider me tainted, but far from it he took me in his arms and wept for the damaged child I had been and we rejoiced at this time of healing and deliverance. Words cannot convey how cleansed and whole I felt and at last this twisted dark deed was set to rest. Thank God I was set free from the perpetrator from this time onwards. Life seemed so much brighter and I could see God's hand in so many aspects of our lives. When we place ourselves under His guidance and protection we have to trust as opportunities come even when we may not feel ready. I am so grateful not to have missed out on this healing time, painful though it was to speak about it after so many years of keeping quiet. Once again, the enemy was lurking to find a way of robbing this joy and freedom newly found through Christ and again tried to spoil things using illness, this seemed my abiding weakness.

It was Christmas time and having my birthday so soon after the festivities, I loved to have a party so all our friends could come to our home and enjoy a celebration. Thinking up a delicious menu and preparing most of it was the best gift of all for me. I left all other details to the rest of the family, but I could be found in the kitchen baking, slicing, mixing and cooking for at least the week before. This was better than even Christmas for me. On this birthday (my 30th) we invited over 50 friends and relatives and selected the theme of famous celebrities.

I was delighted as guests arrived dressed as Billy the Kid, Nell Gwynn complete with oranges; Dolly Parton, Kenny Rogers; Sultans and Harem girls; Vicars, Cowgirls and Pop stars, some more recognizable than others! Everyone was enjoying themselves and entering into the spirit of the party. As the evening went on I began to feel ill with a fever and sore throat, but brushed it aside not wanting anything to spoil this gathering.

Around midnight I told Gordon I was feeling very ill, he could tell I had a high temperature as I was shivering and shaking yet burning up. He quietly helped me to our room and into bed, whilst he saw the party goers wind down and say their goodbyes.

We agreed I probably had flu developing and bed was the best place. I felt bad having to leave all the clearing up to the family but truly felt worse than ever next day. My symptoms also increased with my fever.

Back then in the early 1980s, family doctors still made house calls thankfully. Our doctor examined me and agreed I had a severe case of flu, told me to rest in bed, drink fluids and take regular aspirin was his advice. Getting worse not better after a few days and after more house calls, one from a consultant from the hospital (most unusual), our doctor told Gordon he was ordering an ambulance as my condition had deteriorated worryingly and I needed to be hospitalized. He and the consultant were very troubled I may have had contact with the Legionella bacteria which was killing people in England at that time. Little was known about Legionellae other than it was a fearful bacteria/ pathogen, and my symptoms were fitting into the little they knew about the illness. Skin contagious or air born, no one knew? This made it very worrying. I knew I was dying I felt so ill. I had pneumonia in my lungs, abnormal high fever, and terrible pain on one side of my head, aches and pains everywhere and deathly tired and weak. By the time I was admitted into hospital, my liver and kidneys were failing and I could feel my life slipping way. Medical staff told Gordon to prepare himself for the worst as I may not live through the night. He asked them to call the hospital Chaplain to come and pray for me. Again, God came forth; always His timing is the perfect time. The Chaplain was a gentle Anglican minister we knew well, I can vaguely remember him asking me if I believed God would heal me, I think I mumbled yes! He said I was very sick but still so young and he sensed God has much for me to accomplish in this life and this was not my time to die! John then prayed as he laid gentle hands on my head so softly, instantly I felt power and heat course through my body. It felt I was being irrigated with healing energy an amazing feeling that ended as John withdrew his hands. John was smiling, he also felt the healing power of God and told us later he knew I wouldn't be going to my funeral, but I would be going home to my family.

Medical staff were closely monitoring my condition and became amazed how quickly my liver and kidney function came back to a more normal level; as one doctor said, **'this is a miracle'**! God had taken over my care and slowly I recovered. I had a lengthy stay in hospital to ensure all bacteria had been vanquished by a cocktail of antibiotics. One afternoon a woman I had never seen before arrived at my bedside; she was in England on furlough from the mission field in China and had heard Reverend John speak of me being so very ill in his church service, and how God had miraculously begun to heal me. She felt drawn to come and meet with me and we had a lovely visit. Her descriptions of her work as a missionary truly inspired me. I had never received such wonderful outpouring of 'friends and strangers' love and prayers, before or since. I daily received many cards, flowers and other gifts most I passed onto to the nurses to share with other patients and among themselves. One day it snowed so hard that the roads were impassable and so my sweet, darling son James, aged about twelve years old, walked the four or five miles from our home to the hospital to visit me.

Nurses were shocked he had walked so far as he arrived frozen and tired; clutching a gift for me he had chosen and bought with his own money! He had selected a small glass candy dish. I still have it as it is more precious to me than any gold or silver. He could not wait to give it to me and so walked! Fortunately, the roads began to thaw and his grandfather arrived, so James had a ride home. Despite all the kindness and wonderful medical care, never was anyone so thankful to return home as I was. In that same period eleven people throughout England were infected with the Legionella bacteria and all died except one and that was me. I think I am correct in remembering it was later discovered that the bacteria or spores were air born and formed within unclean water-cooling towers and air conditioning units. These disease carrying spores were then expelled into the air and unsuspecting passersby breathed them in. To this day I do not know where or how I became infected but thank God for the diligent doctors and all the prayers. I became well enough to return to work after about three months, but sadly ever since have had health issues with my lungs, liver and kidneys. In fact, almost one year later I had some severe liver infection which required emergency surgery. My employers were wonderful in always keeping my job for me with full pay and reassuring me to take the time I needed to fully recover. I saw God's hand in this, although the times of being ill and all that meant were awful, I was also protected in the bigger picture. This period of my life taught me so much about prayer. Many people around the country prayed for me each time I was so in need of healing and some were disappointed when my healing was not instantaneous. Yet I was always comforted by sensing the Lord's presence within me and a knowing that I would get better but for whatever bigger reason, the path would be bumpy and long. Our timing is never God's timing and I learned much about patience and waiting, in all these experiences. Suffering and healing is one of the perplexing paradoxes we face. God does not wish or plan for us to suffer but in this world we all fall ill or have accidents. Yet out of these times of suffering God is glorified through His abundant grace and we learn mighty lessons about Him. I thank God for all my times of suffering because this has been my greatest growth spurt in developing my relationship of love, trust and faith with my heavenly Father. He has always been with me every step. I often repeat the following scripture verses when I feel weak or vulnerable;

> *'For it is God who works in you to will and to act in order to fulfill His good purpose.'* Philippians 2: 13 NIV
> and
> *'I can do all things through Christ who strengthens me.'* Philippians 4:13 NIV

After all this anxiety and stress, we had decided to move house again as we felt the need to live somewhere that did not have such sad memories. It was time for a change so God's next phase of his plan could be implemented, but we only understood this in hindsight! Moving down the hill into the Wooburn valley meant changing churches which was hard for us and for Reverend Eric. He was to lose his right hand man, Gordon, who had faithfully served as Parish Warden for 15 years and I was to lose my role as Lay Leader. For two years we attended a Community Church in the valley which was so different to the Anglican way. Gordon and the boys seemed to love it but I struggled with the informality and dismissive and dogmatic attitude towards women in ministry. My lesson this time was to be spent with God teaching me another lesson on humility as I had to let go of everything I held dear in my service to Christ. I needed to learn that we serve at God's behest never our own; He gives and can also take away as all things come from Him. This taught me a painful hard lesson; it was not easy; in fact, I struggled and was often guilty of very ungracious thoughts towards the male leadership. Alongside this, God placed an understanding in my heart that I should not seek to persuade Gordon to leave the church and rejoin the Anglican Church even if this is what I desperately wanted. So inwardly struggling I submitted with gritted teeth! It was not all bad, we made some wonderful new friends and the fellowship was warm and generous with their time and hospitality but this matter of the strong male leadership, dominant and at times dictatorial did not sit well with me but I kept silent. God acted when He knew it was the time and in a short space of a month first our sons and then Gordon had their eyes and hearts opened to how unhealthy and unscriptural some aspects of the leadership was and Gordon made his decision to leave which created the opportunity for me to be honest about my own feelings. For some months I had worshipped at the village Anglican Church when Gordon was on weekend shift work. The Vicar, Reverend Richard was most welcoming and delighted when the whole family began to attend. It was not long before Gordon was encouraged to agree to be nominated for Parish Warden and I was enabled to continue in Lay Leadership by our Bishop. Life was great as far as I was concerned; however, Gordon really missed the relaxed, modern format of worship and the lively worship songs at the Community Church. Yet things among their hierarchy were crumbling and we were thankful to have left when we did. The worship at St Paul's was more Anglo-Catholic than we had experienced before and although I embraced it as a new learning experience, Gordon was not happy at all. Bless him, he stayed for my sake and only grumbled now and again! Our youngest son was still actively engaged in the Youth group although James was reaching an age when he would make his own decisions. At least both boys had a strong grounding in faith and knew their scriptures; also, both had been baptized and confirmed. I was sad to discover that James' negative experience in the Community Church had put him off organized, institutional religion and he found it hard to trust human spiritual leadership again. In his own words to me, at least he believed in God in Christ Jesus and the Bible and promised me he would hold these precious in his heart. Organized church was not for him any longer, but I have no doubt he has continued with this promise.

I had moved up in my helicopter career and was now with another company as a Manager. This meant weekends spent organizing fly-ins to venues like British Grand Prix; Henley Regatta; Ryder Cup Golf Tournament; Luxury automobile media events where multiple helicopters were needed. It was a very busy life but lots of fun especially meeting many sporting and media celebrities. Our sons loved answering the telephone at weekends to find they occasionally were speaking to maybe the current Formula 1 racing champion or on another occasion to one of the Beatles! They found it difficult to understand how their very ordinary mother had calls from such eminent people. Most celebrities were charming and grateful for whatever they needed doing, others could be very rude and a few offensive if they didn't get their own way! For me this was all a great learning curve about the spectrum of human nature. Both sons loved coming along to 'help out' when I had to operate a temporary helipad for a special event. I can imagine the stories they told to their school friends on a Monday morning, no doubt much exaggerated.

On one occasion I won the contract to set up and operate the temporary helipad for the Ryder Cup near Birmingham. Gordon took time off his work to be the radio operator for me and I hired some ex- Royal Marines to operate the fuel truck and assist passengers with bags etc. These three guys had a wonderful sense of humour if a little irreverent at times! On the Saturday evening as we packed up the helipad for the night, one jokingly asked what time would I be starting church parade in the morning being Sunday? Thinking quickly, I sternly replied at 0800 on the dot, all the team to be present and correct or else! As Gordon and I drove back to our hotel, he said you had better prepare for the morning; those guys will try to surprise you. Fortunately, I always travel with my bible so picked out a short reading just in case! Sunday morning dawned bright and dry. As we drove back to the helipad, we came closer to the parking area, I could hear music loudly playing over the field, coming from a little brown tent. Entering the tent with some apprehension I found the three guys smartly attired, with the tent set up like a little church. Somehow, they had acquired a small table with a white cloth and had placed chairs facing the 'Table' on which one fellow had made a rough cross from twigs and twine. The music was coming from a truck radio playing a tape of Elvis singing 'There'll be singing in the chapel'. The short service that followed is one of the most meaningful services I have ever participated in. It was meaningful not just for Gordon and me but for the lads who were tearful by the end, clearly moved. We all were! Each of them prayed aloud and we all felt God's Spirit among us. This is a memory I always treasure. If I had laughed it off and dismissed their inquiry as idle foolishness, we would have missed this special, wonderful holy encounter in the midst of the field. God's moments are all around if we keep our eyes and ears open. It was soon after this time I experienced a dramatic crisis of faith. My working life was spent among the wealthy and famous and their values and ethics were all too often a far cry from what I founded my life upon in my Christian faith walk. Then I met some who told me they too were Christians and yet few lived according to Christ's teachings as far as I understood in our business dealings. I felt torn in two with business loyalties clashing with my personal beliefs and loyalties. At night when sleep eluded me, I faced the harsh reality of 'where did I fit in and who did I want to be deep down'? Businesswoman of the world or woman of God for eternity? As I struggled within my soul for peace, my old enemy of depression came back and brought along nightmares and anxiety. I was plagued with bad headaches and once again my old insecurities came home to roost. I had to take some time off work to find my equilibrium and regain some perspective and it was during this time I had a healing experience of God's love that left me with a restorative strength and courage. I had been praying on this particular morning, and had asked God if there was anything in me, He could love as I felt so worthless. I begged Him to show me His love as I felt so alone and spiritually adrift. As I prayed with my eyes closed, I suddenly **'felt one of my hands being taken hold of and enclosed in a strong, masculine hand'**. I felt no fear and kept my eyes closed knowing this was a spiritual experience and not physical in any way. As I remained still with my heart open to God's touch, love poured into me as an abundant surge. I did not want this precious experience to ever end but of course it did after a few minutes or maybe seconds, I was unaware of time passing at that instant. I sensed this incredible gift of God's grace was given for His purpose, but it certainly came just when I needed it. I had no doubts that I was loved very much by my heavenly Father and He was overcoming the enemy's lies which I had allowed to lodge in my mind. I felt a renewed person and all depressive feelings had left taking with them all negativity and leaving in its place this determination to always seek to serve the Lord no matter where I was or who I was with. A close friend who had a mature sense of belief which I trusted, strongly urged me to make an appointment to talk to a person she knew who had a prayer gift of discerning the spiritual roots of depression and inner pain. Giving this much thought and with a lot of trepidation I made a date for my visit. Many times I nearly called her to cancel but felt this was something I needed to do for my wellbeing. She welcomed me into her study and explained a little how she worked and that I had an hour of her time so to make the most of it. There was no charge as her gift was God given, she told me. She took a short personal history of all the pertinent negative events in my life and then sitting beside me she began to pray quietly for God's Holy Spirit to raise up in me what needed healing, any areas I needed to be set free. Nothing seemed to be happening inside me for ages and I began to feel a little anxious when suddenly all the pain of my mother's death (remember she died just before my first son was born) erupted out of me like lava spewing from a volcano. I even felt I would vomit, as the emotions spewed out. After a while I felt empty, spent of all emotion yet calm. I was just taking stock of what had happened, when she asked why I held so much anger towards my mother. As my mind thought how I had never felt anger towards my mother for dying, only sorrow and grief, a wave of such anger came over me towards my mother for leaving me when I needed her help and guidance the most; as the woman calmly prayed for its release of me; it left me free and at peace. Writing this it almost seems trite but at the time I felt I could self-combust with the forces held within me and then they left and I was at long last free and at peace in a way I had never been before. This whole experience was mind blowing as never once did she ask me about my emotions or in any way initiate my powerful response. I can only explain it by believing God's Spirit was truly at work within us both for good. Something evil was uprooted that day from within me not by any human power or design but spiritually. I left her study feeling like I had had intensive surgery, gotten rid of something so toxic and disabling. The peace of Christ filled my heart and mind in new ways from that day forward. There is so much that is beyond our understanding and too often our scientific, clinical modern thinking disallows us to consider God's healing power and keeps us locked into disabling patterns of thinking and behaviours. From then onwards, my thinking became healthier, less anxiety and insecurity as I discovered my true identity in Christ Jesus my Lord. I was soon to return to work with a new perspective and strong resolve to be true to my faith no matter what. Nothing outwardly had changed but everything inwardly was different for me, newly restored and ready to serve our Almighty God.

It soon became apparent where I was being directed, when our Bishop asked to meet with me. He spoke of my Lay Leadership and how Reverend Richard highly acclaimed my assistance in ministry and said after much prayerful consideration he wanted to put me forward for acceptance for ordained ministry. This would mean going before the three-day Anglican Selection Committee and there was no guarantee they would uphold his recommendation.

This whole idea filled me with fear and trepidation! At this time in the Church of England (1986) women were not able to be ordained to the priesthood, only as deacons. This was not an issue for me as I had never ever thought of myself as priestly material anyway. I loved my role as Lay Leader which I shared with a dear gentleman called George. I promised Bishop Simon I would consider it and talk it over with my family before making any decision.

Gordon was all for it and encouraged me to go ahead and at least try. I decided my decision would rest on the two boys and their responses as it would mean me giving all my free time to study for the next four years.

Within my heart, I was convinced the boys would laugh at the whole idea of me, their mum, becoming ordained and having to attend Oxford theological college for so long. I would still have to earn some money as well!

To my utter amazement when I put the possibility to them at dinner that evening both spoke as one as they said, 'go for it mum, it is what you should do'! What an absolute endorsement that was for me to go ahead and see if my application was acceptable.

By now, I had completed Lay Leader training and been licensed by our Bishop to minister and take church services, including pastoral counselling and also completed the Pastoral Clinical Counselling Course and gave volunteer time to offer people counselling both inside and outside the church; I worked full time and was now considering embarked on another long theological course at Oxford University if accepted. As I write it out it looks such an impossible labour of love, but life just flowed onwards and somehow with my incredible family's support I completed assignments and the years passed by. I confess to not remembering friends and family birthdays as I used to, and rarely could join in with family or friends for meals or celebrations. As my husband once told my college principal 'I have to share our marital bed with my wife and St Augustine or one of the other church fathers'! Any spare moment I was to be found reading and making notes for my next essay or assignment. At around the time of my acceptance for ordination training, a special course was set up for mature students who had other theological credits to train alongside their secular employment with a flexible timetable. This was done through Rewley House an external college attached to Oxford University, allowing us to benefit from probably the very best standard of graduate education in the world. It was a wonderful experience if very tiring and stressful at times. My employers were so good to me allowing me to work less hours and prepared to be so flexible so to allow me to attend lectures in Oxford. God was certainly orchestrating the details and it all worked out in the end. Another life's lesson for me to add to my stockpile, when you allow God to guide and direct the course of one's life, details miraculously fall into place.

We decided to move house again to gain more space and also cut down the time Gordon and myself spent driving to and from our workplaces, as we regretted wasting valuable time taken up commuting. This was to be a blessing in the years ahead as both our future daughters in law moved in at different times and we were also able to offer young people our church accommodation when they were in need. House prices in England had dropped significantly so we could afford a house that once would have been out of reach. Foolishly we did not factor in that mortgage rates were rising at an alarming rate and we would be faced with paying a huge monthly mortgage within a year. Tough financial times were ahead but our heavenly Father never failed us and there was always just enough in the bank account to pay all the bills on time. Gordon took another part time job on his days off to help and I made extra by taking on private clients in need of psychotherapy. Soon I was invited to join our family doctor's medical clinic as their psychotherapist which added to my client list and ensured greater job security. I was still working and studying at theological college and beginning to feel tired. I looked forward eagerly to the end of my studies and promised myself no more training courses for a long time!

Chapter 7

"You, my brothers and sisters, were called to be free. But do not use your freedom to indulge in the flesh; rather, serve one another humbly in love. For the entire law is fulfilled in keeping this one command: Love your neighbour as yourself."

-Galatians 5: 13-14 NIV

Freedom from being a student became a closer reality as I entered my final year of theological studies. The concept of no more assignments or essays, praying for an A or at least B+ was such a lure. As our final year began the wondrous news erupted into the Church of England when General Synod voted for the ordination of women to the priesthood! Freedom indeed for our gender but not welcomed by everyone by any means. Interestingly, middle aged women were the most opposed and outspoken within the church itself, along with some male priests who thought women were the 'devil's spawn'. Then there were the men and women outside the church who took to the hate campaign against us with such energy and spite. There were occasions when it was threatening and unpleasant with tomatoes and eggs being thrown at us outside our churches. The hardest to dismiss with any assertiveness were the cruel spiteful letters and articles printed in the press of the day. It became abundantly clear that the female gender was still cast into a role more suited to the Dark Ages, in many peoples' minds. History would repeat itself sadly when the topic of the right to be openly homosexual hit the world press and swiftly followed on with the hot subject of 'Gay Marriage'. Why do some people find it so hard to love those who are different? Nowhere can I find evidence that the Creator segregated any of His creatures, herding them away from the rest of humanity because of gender or sexual orientation. Is not God the only one who creates life, so why be so afraid, so prejudiced against those who seem 'created different' to yourself?

The first group of women to be priested in the Church of England were those who had been deaconesses for years and I was asked by our Bishop to be his chaplain for the special service. The TV cameras were there in force for this historical event and of course the veggie throwers were out in force too. Those in charge managed to keep everyone out of the building during the service that had no spiritual reason to be there, but it was open season once we all processed outside the great doors. I was caught on camera carrying the Bishop's crozier to pack it away which caused uproar. Looking back, it all seems so ridiculous and such a waste of energy, but for several years it caused both men and women much pain and angst. Once again worldly matters of the flesh divided the Church of God and diverted energy, attention, freedom and action away from the true work of Christ's Commission.

My ordination was splendid; a wondrous ceremony held at Christ Church Cathedral, Oxford along with my college peers and shared with joyful, teary eyed relatives and friends specially invited to witness our momentous occasion. It was Michaelmas and so this would always be remembered along with our wedding anniversary and Gordon's birthday as all close in date.

I felt I had grown wings that day; my heart and spirit soared and joy knew no bounds. I was actually about to be ordained into Holy Orders within the Church of England; I could hardly believe it. It was not to touch my sister and her husband, who refused my invitation to attend. Apparently, *"it was not their thing"!* Even such rudeness did nothing to dent my happy sense of achievement or awe that it was happening at all. My sweet kind Uncle Roy who had encouraged me on my faith journey was there with my aunt, along with other family and friends, plus of course my own wonderful family so proud of their wife and mother.

Our Diocesan Bishop of Oxford, Richard Harries, officiated and when he laid hands on my head at the moment of my ordination, I almost fell forward with the sense of God's power flowing through his hands into my body. It was electric and dynamic and as I stood to walk back to my seat, Bishop Richard gave me a knowing little grin. I sensed he was remembering our private conversation last evening at the Wantage convent as our ordination retreat drew to a close. Each candidate had private conversation and prayer with the Bishop and during our time we had spoken about the Holy Spirit and the importance of coming before God prayerfully and regularly so we might be refilled with God's Spirit to enable our ministry to truly be His will and purpose.

One year later at Michaelmas, I was priested, and on the first Sunday after this ceremony I celebrated my first service of Holy Communion that moved me to tears; it seemed such an incredible privilege to stand and proclaim the sacred words of Christ, asking Him to be present in these Holy gifts;

"Take, eat; this is my body which is given for you. Do this for the remembrance of me"

"Drink this all of you; this is the blood of the new covenant, which is shed for you and for many for the forgiveness of sins. Whenever you drink it, do this in remembrance of me."

I felt so humbled to stand in His presence and serve Him in this time-honoured Eucharistic sacrament. Nothing of this was about me it was all about Christ and His sacrifice for the whole world. Since that first celebration, each time I stand before the Holy Table I sense the unique presence of God's Spirit, so willing to meet with His people and share His gifts with them. It always feels as if we stand on holy ground and should remove our shoes before coming forward to receive the sacraments of bread and wine. Our Bishop had licensed me to serve my parish formation time as curate in a beautiful Berkshire rural area on the edge of a sprawling town. All seemed welcoming at first whilst I was a deacon, then some of our congregation refused to come to the Holy Table to receive the Eucharistic gifts from me if I celebrated that day. Seemingly, in their minds women did not have the right to minister in Christ's role (only men did!) and it was men's right to judge . I refused to make any fuss and quietly served those who did respect my vocation and ordination vows and prayed for those who did not. One particular family, very prominent in the Parish, became vocal about their displeasure in my presence as an ordained minister, although we joined together in the same Bible Group once a week. They treated me with cool off hand disdain, refusing to acknowledge my right under the Diocesan Bishop to officiate as a member of the clergy. It was hugely emotional and healing on the day the couple came forward and humbly knelt at the

Communion rail to receive the Holy gifts from me. After the service they spoke to all gathered to offer repentance and ask for my forgiveness. They went on to explain very apologetically and humbly, how God had given them a strong prophetic understanding of how foolish and sinful they were behaving (their words not mine). They were drawn to reread the verses about how God raised up Deborah to be a Judge in Old Testament times because no faithful man was found to be able to take on this role.

We had been warned that the 'honeymoon euphoria' would not last and within two weeks of arriving in this parish I hit earth with a bump! The training priest to whom I had been entrusted quickly brought me down to earth. He was strongly against the ordination of women and took no time in telling me all I was going to be doing in **'His Parish'** was administration, children's and women's projects! As I began to protest, he yelled at me to keep quiet as I had no voice and would do as I was told. Here I was a mature woman who had led a successful business for years being spoken to like a child. Then I heard a whisper saying, 'humility Kathleen, that is all that is needed'. Here began the hardest days of my adult life, as I learned the pain of humility, of having to lay down my human pride. I quietly did the tasks given and was occasionally surprised to be extended further duties but never any involving leadership; these were the male prerogative only, according to the senior Rector. My initial joy slowly evaporated but I doggedly stayed with as much grace as I could muster. Regrettably, the Rector never came to understand he was making my life very miserable and unfulfilling. One day I asked him why God had led me to be ordained if it was all for naught and his reply was, I heard wrong, as God would never call a woman! He denied me any leadership role of any kind and made his dislike of having a female clergy very clear. It came to a point when our Bishop was so upset about the callous treatment others told him I endured that he offered to move me to another Parish. I was so tempted to accept his kind offer but felt I had to continue in this parish as this was part of my training in humility and perseverance and patience. My decision was the wise one, with hindsight, as I came to understand later how this toughening up was just what I needed for what was coming up as my ministry progressed. Whatever his treatment of me, this rector had many great qualities and gifts as he led others to start up and prosper three church plants in new build communities within the Parish boundaries. I was his only other ordained help and yet he would place untrained laymen to lead these church plants rather than have a woman in leadership. In the years following I came to see he could not share this ministry with any who he felt might overtake him in popularity or share his leadership power. He blamed it on me being a woman, yet he also treated some men in the same way if he felt threatened by them. I long ago forgave him and came to a place of thanking God for the opportunity to develop strength and courage I badly needed. This period taught me how God continues to use the frail and weak humanity, (I count myself among these) and thankfully He does or who could stand in His name? It was not all gloom and doom; I was able to conduct the marriage service for our eldest son, James and his beautiful bride and had an unexpected experience in the church building on the night before their wedding. The church building was steeped in history with parts of it going back to the 10th century. I could sit for hours praying or reflecting, somehow sensing the centuries of sacred worship, the outpouring of prayers that were wrapped within the walls. On the evening before the wedding as I said I was in the church to ensure everything was ready for the joyful celebration, when I knelt before the Holy Table to pray for James and his soon to be wife to find blessing and joy in their marriage, all the things a mother holds in her heart. A quiet sound rather like wings beating started up and I looked around expecting to see birds had got in and were flying about or worse bats! The sound became louder and louder like a vast flock of birds all beating their wings overhead, then it faded away to silence. In my heart I wondered if the sound was the choirs of winged angels warming up their joy and celebration at the coming nuptial ceremony. James and his bride's many years of marriage has had its joys and some sadness, yet they have stood side by side and overcome their adversities together. Could it be because their angels are looking out for them? I like to believe this is, and that I was permitted to sit in on part of the angelic rehearsal!

Since that evening my belief in angels has strengthened. I believe they come in many forms often blending in to our everyday lives, always going about God's work in this world. We do well not to dismiss them out of hand!

In the final year of my theological training, I selected to work my major Placement within a prison setting and set about finding a prison chaplain to accept me for 3 months shadowing their ministry. It was recommended to me by the College Principal that with my psychotherapy qualifications I might find it of interest to work in the British Prison systems at their only Therapeutic Establishment. I gained an appointment to be interviewed by the Governor of the Prison and the Anglican Chaplain on the very day of our Silver Wedding anniversary! Forever we could truthfully claim to have spent our 25th anniversary in prison! Albeit, in the staff dining room. Actually, the food wasn't too bad! Gordon came along with me to give moral support and he was permitted to join in with the lunch interview. It seemed all very informal and their questions were rather odd but at the end of our time I was invited to join the staff team for 3 months, one day a week. I cannot write about the specific details of this time only to say it was both challenging, inspirational and another Divine signal for my future. I only had one conversation after the lunch with the chaplain, when he became terminally ill and was never on duty again.

On my first day on duty, I arrived at the imposing Gate area where I had been previously assured my Visitor's pass would be waiting, to find all the staff denying any knowledge of my arrival. This was a difficult stomach-churning moment for me, was I about to fail this placement before it had begun? Eventually I persuaded someone to call the Governor's office and thankfully he did know about me and remembered I was to be attending each week for 3 months. It took forever but eventually I was on my way into the prison complete with Visitor's Pass and no idea where I was to go or how to get there. A guard walking in my direction made a call on his radio to the Duty Office and found out I was allocated to a certain Wing. He kindly pointed me in the right direction. I do not think I have ever been so scared in my life, what was I thinking of this place gave me the creeps and I wanted to get out as quickly as possible. Then I remembered my father's wisdom of never letting fear get the better of you; so, taking a deep breath I entered said Wing through formidable iron gates, and knocked on the office door. Someone yelled come in, sounding very irritated, which quickly changed to complete and utter amazement as I duly entered. The officer sitting behind the desk went a strange shade of pink as his eyebrows disappeared up into his curly hair. He spluttered something like a welcome and who on 'blank, blank' are you? He was another person who had no idea I was coming and did not seem at all interested or keen that it would be every week. I began to feel very unwanted but then he offered me tea so maybe I was going up in his estimation after all! Ha! I should have known better, as this was yet another test of my mettle. The officer called out someone's name and this person wearing only a tiny, very tight pair of running shorts and very brief Tee shirt came in so swiftly he had to have been listening at the door the whole time. He spoke so informally and casually to the officer I wasn't sure if he was an inmate or an officer out of uniform! They bantered back and forth for a while and then *'short shorts'* rummaged inside a pocket that had to nestle intimately close to all his private parts and pulled out a very crumpled teabag. Dangling it from not so clean fingers he dared me as he said softly, looking me straight in the eye, "tea then for milady"? Every fibre of my being silently screamed nooooooo!! Whilst my treacherous lips said, 'thank you, tea sounds great'! With my reply, the atmosphere in the office lightened and I realized I had just passed some rite of passage and all was going to work out after all. In fact, strange as it might seem, I really enjoyed my time there as the residents began to trust me and spoke of their life journeys that had brought them eventually into this place. I was very privileged to be asked to speak at their Wing gathering towards the end of the placement and felt moved to write a poem as a result of my experiences. I attended a moving Confirmation Service in the prison Chapel with the Bishop confirming eight men. They were allowed to have their families attend the service although families were escorted out immediately it ended. I learn that the mix up about my arrival on that first day was because the chaplain had died suddenly which caused much confusion and so I took Chapel services when I could until a new Chaplain was appointed. I was able to attend the deceased chaplain's funeral which was poignant, as he was clearly deeply appreciated by the prisoners who attended chapel and the staff, and some stood to make mention of how much he had helped them and how he would be missed. Wouldn't we all hope to be so remembered for sharing our gifts and our hearts? This situation left me alone without my mentor to make my own way during the placement; thankfully I had some guidance from the prison psychologist. It certainly toughened me up, no room for shyness or nerves in such ministry. This business of being humbled and toughened up was becoming wearisome! At the end of the placement, I had a long talk with the Principal of my College and then our Bishop, because I was feeling a tug towards prison ministry rather than parish ministry. Both my wise advisors cautioned me that I needed to first complete my three years as a Parish Curate and my continued education programs and then the Bishop would consider my next step.

I was feeling more and more out of step in my secular employment and my heart longed to be in full time ministry. One evening we watched a thought-provoking documentary about the British Prison Service on TV. It showed the overcrowded conditions and the inability to deliver much needed programs and education for the sheer weight of numbers. It gave a very sobering view but left me feeling positive that this was where I should be, not remaining in the rarified world of helicopters and private aeroplanes. After the TV programme I wrote to the Prison Chaplain General for some guidance on application procedures. I also spoke again to the Bishop who was very supportive after having read the report of my major placement, and he said he could see I had some potential for prison ministry. He admitted he could not do it but could see my attraction was genuine and Spirit driven.

It is worth explaining that in the British Prison Service (at least in the 1990s), each institution had to have a full time Anglican Chaplain in post who was then responsible for ensuring each prisoner had access to his/her own denominational or other faith minister. We were also part of the Management team, in which the Anglican Chaplain's input was respected. As someone who valued ecumenism and who had some knowledge of other world faiths, this suited me well. I had some wonderful conversations with ministers of other faiths, along with committed, caring Catholic priests, Franciscan monks, Quakers, Methodists, Salvation Army etc. Some of the Chapel volunteers caused me problems with their refusal to stick to the security protocols; this led in some cases, to be denied future entry since they were blatantly ignoring the rules. Security was the priority, above all else for obvious reasons. These few volunteers who refused to abide by rules were the exception; most brought along faith and realistic expressions of compassion edged with common sense and strong moral values which were in short supply among our prisoner population.

The Chaplain General invited me to attend a preselection Chaplaincy Conference to learn more about the vocation before I formerly applied. It was so interesting and made me even more certain this was to become my fulfilling future. My career in aviation had given me so much experience and personal fulfillment; I had met many interesting people and done many things few people get to experience like flying by helicopter up the River Thames at night seeing London bedecked in jewels with all the lights shining. Attending Paris and Farnborough Airshows and meeting many interesting people not within my usual social circle, even meeting royalty, on a few rare occasions. It had been like a wonderful dream career but now it was time to wake up and do what I had been created to do, to serve my Almighty God as faithfully as possible. I shall always be grateful for this time, so glad I met and worked alongside some wonderful men and women who shared so much of themselves with me and helped shape me into the person I am today. The Bishop also thought it time for a radical change and gave me his blessing and permission to complete my curacy in two years instead of three if I was accepted at the selection Board for Prison Chaplaincy.

The three-day assessment was to prove way more nerve racking than selection for the priesthood! We tackled discussions on ethical thinking, choosing between divergent moral pathways and defending our decisions to our peers. We were given a bible verse and had to stand up on the spot and give a twelve-minute sermon as directed for either a Family Service, Holy Communion service or a Prison Chapel service. Cleary, I did something right because out of twelve candidates I was one of only a small group to be accepted. It felt heaven sent, although I was full of nervous trepidation, I remained convinced it was what I had been born to do. The hardest part was leaving behind my helicopter career. I knew this life was over, but I had met great people and had had incredible experiences, had undertaken projects I never would have thought myself capable of completing. Within ten years, I had worked my way from the bottom rung of the career ladder to being one of very few women close to the very top and it had been a blast most of the time. Now, I had to put it all behind me and become a servant in the true sense of the word. I was to offer my service behind bars among the most broken, hated and reviled members of society and yet it felt so right. Do not get me wrong, I was very afraid, mostly of the unknown, indeed terrified was closer to the truth until I made it through my first week and found my way with Christ always at my side.

I am not able to disclose actual details or names of prisons I served in or of people I met within the walls, but I can tell about experiences initiated by God in Christ, who was to be found everywhere and anywhere, this surprised me at first. I, like so many of the Christian volunteers who came occasionally and gave of their time and energy, thought I was bringing the light of Christ into the prison <u>with me</u>. Well, I was so wrong because He was there all along waiting for us to team up and work together for good. There was darkness and shadows lurking everywhere too, but the prison was certainly not devoid of Light and I met many Christians souls working in there and imprisoned or on remand there, because their humanity had taken them to a bad place, or to make criminal choices; we all know sinister influences abound in this world and how easy it is to be taken in especially when life has been harsh. After all, we are all sinners and only God can ever judge who the worst offender is. This probably sounds weird, but I came to sense that harsh as the environment was, there was a unique honesty to be found among some of those incarcerated rarely found in the outside world. Once the men had accepted their guilt and owned it, honesty became an important principle. Many people asked me how I could work in such a toxic (their word not mine) environment. I would quietly read to them, the passage spoken by the prophet Isaiah that Jesus repeats in Luke's gospel:

> *"The Spirit of the Lord is on me because he has anointed me to proclaim good news to the poor. He has sent me to proclaim freedom for the prisoners and sight to the blind, to set the oppressed free, to proclaim the year of the Lord's favour."* Luke 4: 18-19 NIV.

These verses became my mission statement; they were God's words calling me to service and giving me specific tasks to perform. Can you imagine my joy and delight when inmates would reveal to me, how glad they were to be imprisoned because it was inside prison they found what true freedom is through God and had their spiritual blindness healed. Oh the joy to hear these words spoken over and over during my years as chaplain **"Sister Kathleen, I feel free like never before and I am so happy that I was caught and had this chance in prison to make true repentance and find my way to Jesus."** God is alive and well inside some of the world's most awful prison institutions. There can be nothing like being locked up for 23 hours out of every 24, to focus attention on the big question of who holds the monopoly on the truth and who on lies? Put another way, does God exist and if so do I believe in Him enough to believe He knows me inside out? I witnessed some miraculous times among the despair and senseless violence always present. One event stands out in my memory as being truly amazing. At the huge Victorian-built prison I first served at, one of my daily duties was to visit the inmates in the prison hospital. There was a psychiatric wing and a medical wing and one afternoon I approached the main medical ward down the long hallway to hear mocking male voices calling out loudly for all to be warned for the **"God Squad was coming"**! I was always truly amazed at how intuitive inmates can be to who was in the vicinity and why they had come. I entered the ward to find it full, 6 beds with 4 occupants trying to pretend they were asleep so as to avoid me and 2 eager for some sport with this new chaplain! They soon found out I was up to their fun and games and our conversation turned to more normal topics. One man I shall call him, Michael, a Londoner, told me he was a heroin addict and had not long to live because his heart valves were destroyed by the drugs he had ingested for years; he proudly told me he was not scared of going to hell as he deserved it for the crimes, he had committed to get his drugs. I left soon after that with a mental note to return soon to follow up with Michael. I returned each day and Michael softened in his attitude towards me, less suspicious of me or maybe of what I believed. He had a wonderful sense of humour, never able to be serious for long, so I looked forward to our short times of humorous discussion, but he refused to allow me to speak about God; his story was always he knew he had sinned wickedly and that he deserved to go to hell. No matter how hard I tried to introduce our Saviour, Michael shut down the conversation and would close his eyes and keep quiet until I left his bedside. I had been away for two days and on my return to the medical wing was told that Michael was now in a side room as he was very ill and he had been asking for me. As soon as he heard my footsteps a weakened voice called out to me to hurry up as he wanted to ask me something urgently. He looked so ill but still had his cheeky sense of humour as he made me promise never to disclose what he was going to ask me. My heart sank, prisoners were always trying to get people to bring in contraband products and I got ready to refuse Michael robustly, when I heard his words "could you bring me one of those little prisoner bibles"? I eagerly said yes of course and almost ran back to the chapel where I kept a supply of small Gideon New Testaments (his 'so called' prisoner bible). As I handed one over to him, he sheepishly hid it under his pillow and waved me out of his room.

Next day, Michael looked so much worse and could hardly talk, but was able to tell me he had read the bible all through the night, showing me where he had stopped to underline **John 3 verse 16** and then he said these amazing words to me with tears running down his cheeks, *"Chaplain every story I read in 'ere, it was about me, being blind, being paralysed and afraid, turning my back on this Jesus of yours when I needed him most. Like his friend Peter, I denied him over and over, yet I read how he forgave me, and then I felt in my heart that I loved him and knew for sure he loved me back. Look he says 'ere that he so loved the world, which includes me bad as I am doesn't it? What do you think of that then!?"* What did I think of that, I could hardly speak for the tears in my eyes and the emotion I felt. I wanted to hug him but couldn't, so I prayed quietly, thanking God for all His wonderful guidance of bringing Michael to this moment of knowing Him. As I said, amen, Michael interrupted saying, 'tell him to please forgive me as I would love to meet this Jesus and tell him I loved his book very much!' Michael died soon after this occurred and I was very glad to be able to meet his sister who had tried to look out for him but told me she felt so guilty because she believed she had failed. I told her about his miraculous conversion and all he had said to me and with an amazed look on her face she then revealed the greatest miracle of all, Michael was illiterate, never went to school and could never read or write even his name, yet he read part of the New Testament. Our God is so full of surprises, and we should never underestimate what He can do and will do. I learnt a huge lesson through this experience; I had been so tempted to write those men off on my first visit to the medical wing. The prison held over 3000 prisoners so to try to offer pastoral care and spiritual guidance each day I had to make a choice of which group to drop from my visiting list. I will ever be thankful I kept up my visits to Michael and followed God's agenda not my own. My learning curve was steep as my year's tenure swiftly passed by. I had much help and support from various wonderful members of staff. Each Friday and Saturday I was assisted by a lay chaplain who I later learned was in her 70s yet went around the huge prison with a spring in her step of someone decades younger and always with a positive attitude. She was not afraid of anyone or anything and even our hardest, most challenging inmates treated her with respect. This was in part due to her many years as head teacher of a High School. She was a stern disciplinarian if needed, yet one of the kindest people I ever met, and we became firm friends until her death not that long ago. I could always count on her to do her job to the very best of her ability and to never cut corners or risk security. Yet if she found anyone to be dishonest or hypocritical, she would make them face up to the truth, whether staff member, chapel volunteer or inmate. All too soon, my assistant Chaplain General was telling me I was being transferred to another smaller Victorian prison outside London this time that one that housed Young Offenders.

Just before I was due to visit the new prison to meet the Governor for my introductory interview, I had an accident. Strong wind pushed my open, heavy vehicle door shut with terrific force just as I went to step out of the vehicle onto our driveway. My husband heard the crack as the force of the door hit and broke my nose, bruised my jaw and injured my upper cervical vertebrae. The hospital could not do much for me except pack my nose with gauze offer pain medication and warning about the bruising that would come, plus signs to watch for as I had severe whiplash injuries. I woke up looking like a very swollen panda with green/black bruising around my eyes and face and pain in my nose and neck. I had to take some time off work until the very worst of the bruising disappeared but still looked scary when I arrived at the new prison. Everyone I met would stare at my poor face and ask what happened. I enjoyed telling the young offenders I was a female boxer and they should see the person who lost the match! Word went around and my street cred went sky high! I never had a problem with discipline after that!

This prison was very different to the adult institution, housing boys from 13 years to 18 years old. I felt cast back into my parental role, something many of the inmates had never had. It did not take long to start up a Bible study group at which we had some lively debates on their understanding of the bible and mine! Most of their information came from comics and movies! Although the young men often challenged authority and tried hard to be disruptive, in the Chapel they were fairly well behaved and respectful. They seemed to genuinely appreciate the opportunity to learn something new and engage in open discussion. One Monday evening I invited my Bishop to join us for the evening bible study and he came with some trepidation but left asking if he could come each Monday evening as he had such a great time. He found the questions and discussion refreshing and as he said they helped him regain his perspective on reality. Those times were special for me too. We had several helpers who came one evening a week to help put on an activity and worship service which was well attended mainly due to the cookies and coffee served. The 'lads' as I called them, were all so well behaved and appreciated what was on offer.

Alpha Courses had been running in churches for a several years, and I asked our Prison hierarchy if permission could be granted for me to run a course for the lads. The Prison Service was doing research on how such courses helped improve behaviour in prisons and I got my permission. I then contacted Nicky Gumbel at Holy Trinity Church (the instigator of the Alpha Course) and they kindly sent a team to assist with our initial start-up of the Alpha Course. It was quite an eye opener to that team at how different things needed to be handled and thought out within the prison setting. I feel proud that based on their experience with us 'the Alpha for Prisons' Program eventually was created. I was permitted to have a maximum number of inmates attend and they could also stay and have lunch with us in the chapel. This did not sit well with some of the Wing guards who did not believe inmates should have special treatment. God decided to intervene when one officer kept coming into the chapel to 'check-up'. He was doing this just to disrupt the session as everyone was being very well behaved for they knew I would not put up with any bad behaviour. During a wonderful spiritual time of quiet when some of the teams were praying with the lads, the officer once again started to come in through the chapel door; fortunately, I was standing close by and gently came out closing the door behind me asking him again to please stop disturbing the course. He tried to push past me saying he needed to do a head count as he tried to open the door, it was snatched from his hand and he felt an invisible force push him out into the hallway. He and others could see no one was close enough to push him physically. He was quite shaken and said it must be the chapel ghost (I thought yes, the Holy Ghost) and he disappeared never to trouble us again. Never mess with God! We inside the chapel all knew God was protecting his Alpha Course. However, the young inmates refused to be deterred from coming to the chapel and learning more about their Creator and His mercy and forgiveness. Most of the young offenders had had terrible experiences in foster care and some with their own biological parents, yet most always made excuses for their parents' poor choices and wicked behaviours. The bond between child and parent is almost unbreakable, iron-clad deep down. God blessed many boys as they came to believe in Him and asked me for baptism. Having settled in and getting comfortable with our Chapel programs, it was not too long when once again I was invited to lunch with the Chaplain General and asked if I would agree to a move to another Young Offenders Prison that had a need of someone to start programs and initiatives which were not in place at this time. The new Governor had requested me to join him and who was I to refuse! It was difficult leaving behind so much we had achieved and set in place, but I knew the team of volunteers would help keep things going at least for a while. It was there I found the shining merit in the abilities of the Salvation Army volunteers and I so regretted saying goodbye to these faithful, trustworthy Christian folks who just kept giving and giving of their time and talents whenever there was a need. If the previous Young Offenders Institution was like working in 'Daniel's Lion's Den", this new place was definitely like walking into "Daniel's Fiery Furnace!" It was one of the largest such institutions in Europe at the time and although more modern, at least built in this century it seemed soulless. There were many great dedicated staff and yet nothing ever seemed to go as planned. I discerned there was a spiritual malevolence, an undercurrent of malice and despair that permeated every atom of the place. All levels of staff tried so hard to overcome the apathy and set up healthy programs and education classes; so much goodness was apparent, yet nothing ever seemed to work out as planned. Many staff had serious illnesses and there were always some outbreaks of unrest or violence among the inmates.

I had more sick time than I had ever taken in my life as I kept getting pneumonia. Serving God was an uphill struggle and for the first time I needed all my perseverance and faith to keep going. Good worthy volunteers were hard to come by as they would come once and never return. Bible classes and even the chapel services on a Sunday were always disrupted by bad behaviour, the peace of God seemed far away. One Sunday it all became too much as I led our second service, some boys began to fight in the chapel and refused to stop. I had to take an action I had never taken before and ask the guards to return everyone to their cells immediately. As I went around picking up hymnbooks and bibles that had been thrown and torn, setting chairs up right that had been pushed over or used as a weapon, I sensed in my spirit that this was the end of my prison ministry, this and other sad things made me realize I took this role on believing I had boundless energy and endless zeal but I was now aware of my fragility of being human and reminded I also had a loving family who deserved to be put first for once.

Whilst I served at the Young Offender prison our youngest son, Jonah had married the beautiful daughter of church friends of ours. Once again, I was privileged to marry them, and the bride's father preached the marriage sermon. It was a very happy occasion and all seemed set for a wonderful life together. A few years on they would present us with our beautiful granddaughter. She is the joy of my heart, reminding me in so many ways of me as a child. She is blessed by having a strong Christian influence in her life and knows her God and Saviour well. After their wedding, we left for a well-earned vacation, flying to the west coast of Canada for an Alaskan cruise. Before the cruise we had a week-long trip through the Rockies from Calgary to Vancouver via Banff, the Columbia Icefield, Jasper, Kelowna and finally our cruise ship in Vancouver harbour. It was well organized and comfortable with many interesting stops each day. On day three on the way to Jasper we stopped for a raft ride down the Frasier river rapids. It all seemed like fun until it started. I was in a vulnerable seat on the raft and was getting soaked with freezing glacial melt water each time we rode a rapid and some were rough! By the time the ride ended I was shivering with cold and soaked to the skin, no one warned me about hyperthermia and within a few hours I was very ill with a high fever and yet shivering as though I would never feel warm again. When we arrived at our stop for that night I went straight to bed after a hot bath and battled the fever all night. Gordon went to speak with the tour guide who showed little compassion or interest that I was ill. She told him, either I kept up with everyone or stayed behind and took the train to Vancouver. I wasn't about to be abandoned in the middle of the Rockies so I tried valiantly to keep up, dosed with Tylenol at regular intervals, praying to hang on so I could just get on the ship! This story does not end happily as I did get on the cruise with Gordon but during the first night had to be taken to the Medical Bay and hospitalized as I was very ill by now with my fever climbing dangerously high. On the third morning the ship docked at Juneau and I was taken by Fire Truck to the hospital where I remained for about ten days. Poor Gordon had to miss his holiday and spent it in the lodge attached to the hospital for families. I had bacterial pneumonia and suspected meningitis and when they discharged me to fly home one of my lungs was collapsed. Gordon spent day after day either by my bedside or watching Christian TV programs to keep him strong to trust and believe I would recover. Another attack by the enemy but the only forfeit was we missed out seeing Alaska. In 2012 we made up for this and took and completed another cruise up the Inside Passage to Alaska.

I arrived back in England with one collapsed lung, much weakened and not feeling at my best or strongest to continue working in the harsh environment of the with many challenges ahead.

So much happened around this time; Gordon's job came to an abrupt end when the airline he had worked with for over 25 years suddenly announced the closure of the London office. He was offered an early retirement package that seemed fair to accept. God never promises us an easy journey through this life and the unexpected is always hovering, unseen in the background. Our sons were both married to wonderful young women and had their own homes and lives. We had a house much too large for the two of us and both sensed we were about to face a major change. Gordon did not want to retire as he loved being part of the hum of aviation and had taken on another job setting up an aircrew briefing office for a major airline, at the same time I moved on to the third posting to a Prison establishment.

Chapter 8

"Therefore go and make disciples of all nations, baptizing them in the name of the Father and of the Son and of the Holy Spirit, and teaching them to obey everything I have commanded you."

-Matthew 28:18-20. NIV

Whilst I was still working for the helicopter industry, years before serving in the Prison Service, I had a very vivid dream or vision of Gordon and me ministering together in Canada. I saw an image of a large white building set upon emerald green grass. Gordon had the role of bringing in the lost and telling them about the Good News of Christ, whilst my role seemed to be pastoral, one of healing prayers for the sick, wounded and dying. I awoke with a sense this dream was meant to be understood as prophetic. Since that time, we kept looking for signs to move on, to move out to another place, another country even. No such signs came and the years passed and I, though never forgetting the dream or its vivid impression, began to believe it had only been a dream and nothing more. Oh, me of little faith!! In God's timing, a thousand years is but a year and a year is a thousand! I didn't wait a thousand years, but it was a long time, twenty years or so!

So here we found ourselves with Gordon semi- retired at least, and me knowing my days of Prison service were drawing to a close, yet nothing presented itself as the next step. What should we do, stay as we are? What we forgot to do of course was pray for God's guidance for our next step. How easy it is to remind others to *'take it to the Lord in prayer'* as the line of that lovely hymn "What a Friend We Have in Jesus' goes. It took us weeks to remember how we prayed for everyone else but neglected to pray for our own lives. Once we remembered and took our dilemma to the Lord, the answer came quickly although it did not instantly fill my heart with promise and joy, quite the reverse. Each month I received the Anglican Times newspaper and this edition, Gordon got to read first. I came home to see it open at a page near the back with an arrow marking the advertisement he wanted me to read. It was headed up 'ANGLICAN PRIESTS NEEDED FOR DIOCESE OF THE ARCTIC, CANADA'! Neither Gordon nor I were that keen on anywhere too cold, in fact we had spoken of moving to Florida or the Caribbean! It transpired God has other ideas for us! Gordon seemed adamant I was to apply to the Diocesan Anglican Bishop of the Arctic. I argued that only male priests would be interviewed for such an isolated, environment and anyway I hated the thought of snow, ice and perpetual night for months on end. There was not one shred of optimism or positivity in my soul about any potential. I was aghast that Gordon was giving it any credence. We said nothing to our family or friends about this until we had some suggestion of an affirmative response from Canada. The response came when the Diocesan Bishop to the Arctic, Chris called us having received my application. He waved aside any misgivings I had being a female priest and only afterwards did I wake up to the fact I had just been interviewed for a position in *"the Arctic"!* I was told another prison chaplain had also been interviewed and if our immigration process went well the four of us (two married couples) would take up vacancies to lead mission parishes somewhere in the western part of the Diocese, way up north in Canada. Gordon immediately got out the world atlas and spent a while finding the correct part of the world. It looked frighteningly uninhabited with very few roads and even fewer settlements, but it did have a capitol town which we discovered was named, Yellowknife and we came to know it very well. Not yet though, all we had to go on were our local library's very few books written about the high Arctic in about the 1800s. Could we really do this? Who were we kidding! Neither of us was a camping nor hunting enthusiast who enjoyed living off the land! I loved wide open countryside and seeing animals in their natural environment but needed to go home to sleep under a proper roof, with a fridge, hot water and power points! Any microcosm of adventure spirit within me had an unusual boost when a surprising encouragement came along in the form of the British Press and TV documentary makers. I began to receive call after call from journalists and documentary producers wanting to follow my footsteps into this unique region of the world. Once they discovered I wasn't going to be at the North Pole or preaching to polar bears and seals most of them lost interest, but a few persisted and once I settled into our new northern home a British Sunday Supplement magazine photographer came to follow me over a typical day in the life of a new mission Anglican female priest. Nothing was ever published as some celebrity presented with more interesting news than I offered. All my poses on a loaned snow machine were for nothing, some you win and mostly you lose!!!

This was still in the future. Bishop Chris ended his phone call with the news that I was to attend a day's gathering in a Leicester Anglican church to meet the man who was

Archdeacon for the Diocese of the Arctic who would informally interview me and Gordon to discern if we would cope with the life and ministry up in the far north. We would also meet the Fellowship group who would generously finance our move to the Arctic. They were very generous and covered our moving expenses for our household items and also our Immigration costs. This move entailed us actually immigrating to Canada and beginning a process that ended when we became Canadian citizens five years after we landed in Toronto. This whole enterprise led to us leaving everything behind in England. The Archdeacon's interview technique put us at ease very quickly as he had a great sense of humour. He did not know where we would be posted but it was very obvious, he would be a great support and mentor. He spent a while asking me different questions about how I thought I would deal with suicides, as the far north of Canada sadly has more suicides especially among young people than anywhere else in the world. I was able to say I had some experience as suicide was something that occurred in the prisons, I served in. He gave us a quick overview of the way of life and some of the cultural customs we could expect. All this was very helpful as we had so many questions. We began the slow process of immigration; unaware it would take over a year until we could travel to Canada as Permanent Residents. We had to have medicals and complete forms to be sent to the Canadian Embassy together with the required payment. Bishop Chris called one day to ask if we had any news on an arrival date. The answer was as usual, no, we still had no news. We had our house up for sale, but still had not given notice to our employers. Bishop Chris told me he would like us to meet up with a couple now ministering in an Anglican parish in the Guildford Diocese to hear from them about life in the northern Inuit community of Coppermine or to called by the Inuit, Kugluktuk. Seemingly, this is where he would be posting me (us) once we arrived. I would get help from other clergy to learn Inuktitut so I could preach and take services in the indigenous language. This sounded very ambitious, others had spent their lifetime of ministry among the Inuit and Aboriginal peoples of northern Canada and had over time picked up the local dialects. Whereas I was expected to speak and understand with a fluency, that would take years to accomplish. You never argue with your Bishop, so I kept quiet about these misgivings and made contact with the couple in Guildford as directed. On the agreed day of our visit, they warmly welcomed us for supper and initially the get together went well. Then Gordon began to ask questions about their family life and mission service in Kugluktuk. They spoke of the warmth of the people and their love for Christ; their generosity and willingness to help. Then he began on the specifics; the harsh isolation, living perched on the edge of the Arctic Ocean; the high dependency on alcohol and drugs by all ages and its damage and destruction to families and the whole community; the high numbers of suicides, overdoses and hunting fatalities. The expense of purchasing the essentials for living was exorbitant, as was the cost for travelling out to Yellowknife, for medical, dental and the like, for any appointments and treatment. We were to soon understand how this picture described all communities up north, some being more ensnared than others. Up until now all he told us met with my assessment from what I had read and gleaned from the Internet and rare books I found in our local library. Yet this was new to Gordon's ears and he became quieter and paler by the minute as the descriptive words rolled from the minister's lips! Then he continued by saying how with no funeral company available it could be left to us to go out on the snow-covered tundra in winter to find and bring home a dead person and prepare them for burial. He was not short on describing every detail painting a vivid image for us to hold in our minds forever. Gordon had reached his limit at this and stood up grasping my hand as he thanked the couple for the meal and we left swiftly. I was dragged along to where we parked our vehicle. Gordon sat for a while with his head on the steering wheel, eventually looking across at me saying, he was so sorry, but he could not do this. This proposed new life was a step too far and too big for him. I had to accept this and told him it also filled me with trepidation, I have always been the more adventurous of the two of us, but my imagination did not stretch to me being a part of this kind of life. I knew I did not have the stamina or physical strength that would be required and did wonder why God had permitted us to get so far down this path if it was so wrong! The next day, filled with regret, I called Bishop Chris to withdraw my application. Gordon and I felt thankful we had the reality check before the immigration process went further. Our sons were aghast when we shared the insights with them, saying in various descriptive ways we need our heads examining to even imagine living in such conditions. Despite all this, something stopped me halting the Government process and refused to allow me to remove our house from the Realtor's listing.

We had many restless days and nights trying to decipher what to do next. No other plans came to mind, no alternatives with our names on them seemed to exist and we were left in limbo for about two weeks. On an evening I was out, Gordon took a call from Bishop Chris who had done lots of his own heart searching and told my husband about another Parish just within the Diocese of the Arctic that had become available. It was a community of 2,500 mainly aboriginal Canadians with a large Federal Parks and Forestry Department, a small airport with its own airline, a Community Hospital, a College, schools, two prisons and other many services. I was not party to their conversation that night but whatever Bishop Chris told Gordon it put his mind at rest and he said he would be happy to live in this place if I was. It was the mention of an airport that sold it to Gordon!

Once again God had revealed a piece more of his agenda and once it was rolled out, the pieces all fell into place. I was relieved and delighted with this offer and readily accepted the generous second chance. This was my answer as to why I had not changed our plans to sell the house or to keep the immigration process moving. God intended us to take up a ministry in this northern outpost and needed us to see clearly our own motives within our own human limitations. This change would be tough enough without any false bravado from either of us. Jonah expressed mixed emotions at our plans to leave England, he would miss us very much as we would miss him, but he and his wife were excited at visiting this new part of Canada. James was firmly in denial that we would leave and was adamant we would not go. He and his wife had just adopted our darling first grandchild and he could not imagine we would not stay for him. This would prove to be one of the hardest things in all this change. Had we really counted the cost of leaving behind all the daily joys and experiences of being with our own family? We spoke often of the ease of travel and opportunities for visits back and forth, but the reality was relationships were strained and our family ties suffered. Much has been written about the negative fallout and effect upon the children of ministers, who often feel left out or left behind whilst parents are busy 'following the Lord'. I believe as healthy adults, both parents and adult children, should follow their own call, using the freedom of choice we all have to follow the path we see before us. We raised our sons to have that freedom and Jonah has used his in his choices and we hope so has James. We shall carry regrets to our grave that we missed out on watching our grandsons and granddaughter grow up. Yet would we have seen much more of them had we stayed in England? Everyone leads such busy lives these days.

Time passed so slowly once we had made our decision and it was to be a full year before immigration became a reality. We took the decision about 6 months before all this to have a brief visit to meet Bishop Chris in person in Yellowknife and then fly on to Fort Smith to meet those destined to become our parishioners and neighbours. Plus, we were most curious about the community. It was a very long stressful journey for five days stay but well worth it. We flew from London Heathrow Airport to Edmonton, Alberta stayed one night and then flew on to Yellowknife the next day to a warm welcome by Bishop Chris. He seemed delighted to have 'two newbies' to show around the North West Territories capitol, He had such pride in his northern home it was tangible as he drove us around; pointing out the large General hospital, shops, cinema and the colourful houseboats on the lake. Yellowknife sits on the shore of the Great Slave Lake, the next largest lake after The Canadian Great Lakes. It is a very beautiful place in the summer and fall, with sparkling waters and varied colours in the trees and vegetation. Everywhere one looked there were huge rocks, part of the Great Canadian Shield. Building land was limited because of the rocks and so house prices were incredibly high. We had one night with him and his wife before flying south across the Great Slave Lake to Fort Smith in one of the family-owned aircraft. It was exciting to fly over such huge distances of nothing but the bush or water! No other settlements between and then suddenly carved out of the trees appeared the paved runway of Fort Smith Airport. It seemed to exist in glorious isolation until one could identify one road leading into the small town. The terminal building was small and crowded with our welcoming committee. I felt like the Queen must have felt on her visit here many years before! Everyone hugged us and joyfully shared the warmth of their reception. It was clear they were delighted we had made this effort to meet them before commencing formal duties. The Archdeacon arrived in his vehicle having driven the 300 kilometres from the closest community of Hay River where he lived. He was to spend the next two days with us staying in the rectory and guiding us around the town. We were getting fuzzy headed with jet lag, but the bubbly joy kept us going until we arrived at the very comfortable, cozy rectory and thankfully naptime was called. After some much needed sleep we were ready for the meet and greet Potluck supper. On the short walk over to the Parish Hall we learned of its interesting history. Once it had housed the Hudson Bay factor's offices where the trappers came to sell their furs and skins, a main source of wealth in the last century. When the Hudson Bay ceased this form of trading, they gave the building to the Anglican Church for a nominal sum. So, from furs to suppers, both keeping folks warm and jolly! This felt a good place to make our new home and we became excited for the process to begin. One huge bonus we had yet to realize was being in the right place to witness the incredible display of The Northern Light or Aurora Borealis! We never tired of the spectacular light show night after night. We met many wonderful people at our welcome Potluck supper that evening as we sampled the amazing variety of home cooked dishes. One thing was certain we would never starve here. The church building, St John's, was next door and a pretty church, hand built out of wood gleaned from everywhere and anywhere.

Money had been sent from England in the 1800s to ensure the Anglicans had their own sacred place of worship. As we sank into bed in what would become our bedroom for twelve years, we both acclaimed it felt good to be here and we could make this our home for however long God ordained it. Knowing where we would be living and ministering made our waiting very difficult and impatience had to be daily set aside as we waited for word on Immigration and on finding a buyer for the house. Only weeks before a buyer was found, disaster hit as one day; one morning a loud thump shook the garage and the house. The garbage truck brakes had failed resulting in the driver hitting the side of our garage attached to the house. The damage was considerable but again God saw us through. Our insurers made certain the Council paid every penny of the cost of rebuilding and found us a construction firm who did such a great job that nobody could tell where the old or new wall started and finished. We were truly blessed in what began as a tragedy. Buyers appeared just as the work was completed and were not phased at all but rather were glad, they now had a strong new wall on one side of the house. We had our house sale completed but where were our Immigration visas? It was now close to the end of March 2001 and we had to move out within a week, but where could we go? The Christian Fellowship Group in Leicester had told us to have an international removal firm of our choice come and pack up all the household items we needed to take to Canada. They were booked for the end of the month, but still no Canadian visas arrived. We would soon have no jobs, no home and nowhere to go. Yes, I had learned something so I prayed fervently for a sign, a direction, anything that would bring comfort. Soon after praying, I had to drive over to a friend to drop something off for her and on my way back I passed a small local hotel. I slowed down sensing an inner need to turn into their carpark. Why was I here? Easter came to mind coming up in eight days' time but why would I think of Easter right now? Then it came as clear as clear, I had been directed here to book a room for us to move into at the end of the week. I explained to the receptionist that I did not know how long we needed to stay as we would be immigrating to Canada as soon as the paperwork came through. However, I found myself telling her, I thought we would be leaving two days before Good Friday. She was so interested in why we were going, asking all sorts of questions and on finding out we were locals, gave us an exceptional room rate and a beautiful room in a lovely quiet corner. Happier now we had somewhere to move to still close to the family, and a sense of the timing of our departure, I raced home eager to share this with Gordon. He had his own news to share. He had called the Canadian Embassy in London feeling exasperated at having no news. They put him through to a most helpful person who on hearing about our application said he knew all about us and our paperwork was on his desk ready for his signature and he would make sure to have it couriered to us before Good Friday. Take it to the Lord in prayer folks it is the only way to gain answers and guidance.

I called Bishop Chris and said I would be at St John's for Easter day and we were! All kinds of obstacles came onto our path leading up to our departure but by keeping faithful in our trust of the Lord, we ensured His assistance in all the important details, so they fell into place. We landed in Fort Smith on Maundy Thursday just before lunch time to a rapturous welcome this time. One couple handed me the keys of their second vehicle saying use it as long as you like until you sort out your own. I didn't even know their name at that point. Kindness flowed from all directions, it overwhelmed us. We had left behind everything, in England, yet found another family waiting in Canada to receive us into their hearts. It was humbling and filled us with such warmth and thankfulness! One of the pilots who flew us to the airport, in talking to Gordon found out about his long career in commercial aviation and almost dragged him into the President's office, saying for him to meet and speak to Gordon; he kept saying over and over, Gordon is our answer to prayer. This resulted in Gordon being offered a role in the airline. He had been prepared for his aviation career to be over, once he left England and had committed himself to helping out around the church for the future. **"God's ways are not our ways, He always knows our needs and gives way more abundantly than we could ever ask or imagine."**

There was so much to rejoice about that Easter Holy day in 2001. I celebrated Holy Communion for the first time in our little wooden church set on the edge of the Boreal forest, alongside the only main road. The congregation sang with such joy that morning as we shared God's holy gifts at His Holy Table. I felt 'home'! It never seemed like I was from somewhere else; there was a familiarity to life and its rhythm continued uninterrupted by our presence. A place opened for us and we fit it perfectly. Much of the North West Territories reminded me of East Africa and this helped me feel right at home. The sense of wide opened spaces, home to wild animals, living within the land of the aboriginal peoples that belonged to them for centuries before white people appeared, it was so familiar and yet different too. Gordon admitted sometime later, it took him longer to settle than he thought it would. He had lived for a time as a teenager, in Saskatchewan so should be more familiar to Canada than me. It was the total isolation that he found hard. I struggled with this too when faced with the first major forest fires. We were all alone in one sense; although with 2,500 people reliant on each other for everything, we were never alone, and always within the heart of our Father in heaven. The aboriginal peoples welcomed us and were so interested in our journey to get from our old life to here. On Easter Monday, we found the newest member of our family when we visited the Animal Shelter.

We both wanted a dog, and it had to be a big dog! The woman who showed us around tried to interest us in an Alsatian puppy, she felt would be right for us. However, I kept going back to the enclosure that held the most beautiful dog we had ever set eyes on, a German Shepherd, husky, wolf cub crossbred. The dog sat quietly looking at me as if we belonged together. I asked to be let into her enclosure. The shelter woman was very cautious as the dog was bred to be a working dog, to pull a sled and had never been trained to be a pet. Later the woman confessed she feared the dog might tear my throat out, but I insisted on going in, this was definitely our new dog. I slowly approached the animal allowing her to get used to my scent. Once I was near, she leaned into me and placed her head against my hand. She loved me rubbing her ears and then I spoke saying to her "your name is Sacha, you belong with us": On saying the name '**Sacha**', she responded by throwing back her head and giving a loud wolf howl. It sounded as if she agreed! Sacha has been our delight and joy for the 14 years we had her. She was so intelligent it took no time to house train her and socialize her; she loved people and children especially. In all the years we had her she only growled twice at dubious characters and never snatched food, snapped or snarled. She was a big softy, yet could be wayward, and had a Houdini trait of releasing herself from her harness if she felt bored. People in the town knew her well so when she went walkabout, they would tie her up and call me to collect her. Sacha became a preacher's dream. She was always chained outside the rectory if we went out anywhere; one Sunday she was outside as the Gospel was read from St. John. It was about Jesus being the good shepherd and how His sheep always know His voice, as I commented on this scripture and repeated it for emphasis, Sacha gave a loud affirming howl as if to say, 'yes and I recognize your voice'! She never did this again only this once. We also gave a home to the prettiest calico kitten that grew into a huge cat with awesome attitude. In no time Tigger had Sacha well trained; on a wet or snowy day if both were outside, Tigger made certain she was sheltered in the dog kennel leaving Sacha half in half out! Their antics kept us amused and often exasperated. One Sunday just before I stepped to the Holy Table for Communion Tigger appeared from under the pews, jumped up onto the Holy Table and curled herself around the Brass Cross. I was mortified and rushed to remove her just as our oldest congregant called out to me to leave her be! She continued loudly, 'urging how we all should be curled around the foot of the cross like Tigger!' My pets presented great teaching moments. Both were definitely God's special provision for us. Sacha being so clearly a working dog, the Aboriginal people loved to ask about how we came to have her and thought it amazing that I could control this huge dog as we walked the riverside trails together. Sometimes I couldn't control her and she would get away and once this happened close to the road and she became caught up under the wheels of a big truck. Fortunately, the driver was going slowly but one of his big wheels went over her back. This had to be the end I thought as with tears running down my cheeks, I ran over to her. Seeing me she tried to stand but one hindquarter kept giving way. The truck driver was as inconsolable as me and carried her to his truck bed and drove us home to the rectory. I repeated that he was not to blame in anyway it could not be avoided. He helped me get Sacha inside and left. I sat on the floor beside her and prayed for her to be restored completely, laying hands upon her gently. She closed her eyes and seemed to sleep, so I went to call Gordon to let him know of the accident. We were still talking on the phone when I felt her cold nose against my leg, she was limping but able to walk with no whimpering or sign of pain; although the vet checked her thoroughly when he came to town, taking x-rays, he found no sign of any serious damage. The driver and I had witnessed the truck roll over her with one wheel, yet she was whole! Another miracle to praise our wonderful God for! Sacha became well known for her 'accidents' but she had a gentle manner and was our faithful friend for many years. Towards the end of our time in the north, one morning Gordon had left for work, placing Sacha outside on her chain as usual outside the kitchen window. I heard her suddenly begin a frenzied howling and barking, as I had never heard before, I rapped on the window to no avail, she just got more frenzied. I was still in my nightdress and did not have my spectacles close by (I have very poor sight without them) so ran to the back of the rectory to see if anyone was in our yard frightening her. What I saw took my breath away! A large black bear was just in the tree line between our yard and the cemetery and did not look too happy with Sacha threatening it with all her barking and noise. Sacha would stand no chance in an attack as she was firmly held captive by her chain. With no thought at all, except I had to rescue my beloved dog, I ran outside (still no spectacles, with limited sight and still dressed only in a short nightdress). As I fumbled to undo the chain Sacha was pulling and dancing about, making it even harder for me as I tried to focus on where the bear was in relation to us. I could only see a large black blob that seemed to get closer just as Sacha came loose from her chain and together, we ran through the front door which I locked firmly behind me as I began to shiver and shake, as fear took hold of me. The bear was very close to the house by now and we were safe inside just in time. The bear had to be trapped by Park Rangers and hopefully they released it somewhere far outside the town. Many motorists on their way to work missed seeing the bear as they were too amazed to see me in my nightdress!! It was probably time we left town!

My original agreement with the diocese was for a three-year term, but we ended up staying for over eleven years which tells how much we felt at home. It felt home right away to me and Gordon quickly settled in especially once he was back working within aviation. The owners of the airline were parishioners at St John's and very generous in helping any residents who needed to get flown on one of their routes, for anything urgent. There was a true spirit of 'loving your neighbour' since we all relied on one another for everything. It took 16 hours to drive to Edmonton and almost 3 hours to drive to our nearest community through boreal forest on a dusty, bumpy paved road for half the distance and a very bumpy, dusty gravel road the rest of the way. One could always expect to find huge bison meandering down the middle of the road somewhere along its length, and often wolves and bears could be spotted. Patience was needed since you could not barge past the bison, they were too big and when in rut, the males could charge at your vehicle. Imagine an animal the size of an elephant charging towards you head down with his big curved horns! We experienced that once and it was the stuff of nightmares. Thankfully Gordon put his foot hard on the gas pedal and we 'fishtailed' out of range. If I had been driving, I think I would have frozen and probably been badly injured or at least shaken up. Life was so different from England. Imagine anywhere else in the world, where seeing me struggle with a very large parcel I had collected from the Post Office an unknown man comes up and offers to drive it to the rectory and leave it outside for me. Kindness and thoughtfulness occurred every day in many guises. I hope we reciprocated in the same measure we received! Unknown people would stop at the rectory with wild meat and bones for Sacha; wild moose or caribou meat and local fish, home baking and vegetables for us, generosity flowed and we felt humbled and very blessed. I had started using my psychotherapy experience by helping people suffering with bereavement, depression and anxiety etc. There were two prisons in the community, so it wasn't long before I was invited to go on a regular basis to counsel the inmates. This experience opened my eyes to the reality of the struggles aboriginals had as they tried to adjust to living in two cultures. The casualties I met could not make the adjustments and fell between the cracks so often. Alcohol and drugs had become their coping balm for their wounds and many fell in deep despair enough to take their own life in suicide or make multiple attempts. As I began to initiate courses for those ensnared in alcoholism, drug abuse and mental illness and suicidal ideation I realised I needed more training than my Pastoral Counselling courses had given as too often I felt out of my depth. I was fortunate to be offered a scholarship to study for a Bachelor's degree in Science majoring in Psychology and then went on to gain a Master's degree in Science. These gave me greater sense of being resourced, but I learned far more from the clients as they shared their struggles so courageously. I was planning to go further and gain my Doctorate but just ran out of steam and money and felt I had studied enough. The north is a kind and generous place if you were blessed with a stable lifestyle and a well rooted sense of self confidence. Otherwise, I sensed a dark place underneath which sought out the weak and vulnerable; those who lived self-defeating lives and had no sense of God's heart of love, forgiveness and His power to set the captive free. It wasn't only aboriginals who fell by the wayside, some others did too. It could be too harsh and isolating for those who craved urban hustle and bustle.

It took a few years to begin to understand this was not utopia; my first impressions were too idealistic. Having said that, it was full of many good people, who worked hard, unstintingly volunteering in an effort to meet the needs that arose. In any crisis or accident, the whole community came together in strength and solidarity. When people live in such isolation there is nowhere to hide and everyone knew everyone's business or thought they did. For those who valued privacy above all else, this made it untenable for them and so they left if they could.

Church life was an important integral part for many of the people. Beside the Anglican Church there was the Pentecostal Church and an enormous Catholic Church building (built when this town was going to be the capitol). It was set at the very heart of the little town and had a positive presence as one drove or walked up the main street. It stood as a visual reminder that God is at the centre of our lives whether we recognize Him or not. Inside it was simple in decoration and yet beautiful. I took many services there over the years, as funerals and other well attended services and events were held there regardless of denomination. That generous spirit showing itself. It was as difficult to get Catholic priests as Anglicans up north so in their times of having no one, I would be asked by the Catholic bishop to take a funeral for them. In this way I was so blessed to be able to forge strong links to all sections of our community.

I met a dear Christian senior who had come north many years before to serve alongside her pastor husband. They came from a very strict Baptist group in the USA. He refused to acknowledge me as a woman pastor, but she was a gentle, deeply spiritual person who taught me much about the north that one could not see with the naked eye. She discerned that the vast area was gripped in some kind of spiritual power encounter between God and His enemy and this was one major reason for so much despair and suicides which decimated many families. I found myself sometimes wondering if this was not all too fanciful at times, but I was soon to be given a fresh understanding on this subject. Soon after our arrival, Gordon and I were invited to attend the grand opening of The Miracle Channel in Lethbridge, Alberta. They were celebrating having gained a hard-won license to broadcast only Christian programs. We were very excited to travel south and looked forward to hearing some good teaching from the speakers. The keynote speaker on the first morning was from England and known for his prophetic gifts, which had us all wondering, what he had to say to us. After being introduced, he stunned the hosts by saying before he began his talk, he had sensed God tell him to do something extra special! Now we were all stunned! Especially when he called all those ministers and pastors present from the north of Canada to stand up! I felt Gordon dig me in the ribs, nudging me hard to stand up. I saw many people stood so felt comfortable joining them. (Comfort in numbers!) Not for long, as he quickly qualified his request saying only those from the far north of Canada should remain standing the rest must sit down. This left six of us standing and he brought us to the front and began to speak a strong word of prophesy over us about how the north was raising committed Christians who would show the world how to truly follow Christ in Spirit and in truth. He asserted how our role was to preach the Word of God in all situations and opportunities. He used way more words but that is what I took into my heart with goosebumps on my arms as I listened to him. He then quietened and we began to turn back to our seats. Imagine my pulse rate rising as I felt him hold me back, as the other five sat back down. He looked directly into my eyes and spoke spiritual facts about my ministry he could not possibly know in any human sense. He told me God had sent me to serve in a difficult place where the enemy would try to harm me. I had not spoken to a soul since arriving. Apart from my husband, I knew nobody here. All he spoke came about and I went through some very hard experiences, with accidents and illness top of the list. But through it all I always sensed God was with me and He brought me through each hazard still standing, holding me in place and allowing no lasting harm to hurt me. In the following years, a deeply spiritual Catholic priest came to our little community and shared many things with me that he had experienced in his long years in ministry things that made sense of what the prophetic speaker had said to me. There was a growing release of the Holy Spirit in the far north among the church but there was also sinister resistance and practices that created dramatic power encounters in the spiritual realms. Those in the prisons who wanted to attend church could come to one of the services each Sunday and our congregation always warmly welcomed those who took this opportunity. Some were baptized and confirmed which strengthened ties about being part of a wider family of God, for those who had no earthly family.

I was greatly honoured one year to receive the Town of Fort Smith's Citizen of the Year Award, not feeling I had done anything of any significance! I was invited to be the Chairperson of the Hospital Ethics Committee and gladly accepted. Medical ethics has been an abiding deep interest to me. It was an interesting subject when I took my post graduate studies (Bachelor's and Master's degrees in Science). It was through the Ethics Committee I met a new friend who nursed at the Medical Clinic. Kate became like a daughter to us and was a frequent visitor to our home. She would housesit when we went on vacation or on education leave and the love she had for Tigger and Sacha was warmly reciprocated by the two pets. In fact, when we finally left the north, Kate drove our vehicle with Sacha in the back seat all the way to Prince Edward Island. We flew east after a trip through British Columbia and Alaska.

Three years quickly rolled by and no one from the Diocesan office called to say, *"are you leaving us now?"* So I stayed and stayed and the years went past so quickly. It was a joyful day when our new Diocesan Bishop, Andrew Atagataluk spoke with us about Gordon being ordained to Parish Deacon in recognition of all his ministry especially outreach among the aboriginal men. This meant a lot to Gordon in having this validation from our Diocesan Bishop.

Our congregation increased in numbers each Sunday with many young families joining us. There was a small youth group and Sunday School that encouraged us all. Every couple of years Edmonton hosted a popular YC Conference at the Rexall Place. During our time of having a youth group, interest developed in taking them to this Youth Conference. Inevitably, it fell to Gordon and me to chaperone and lead them. I had reserved a hotel suite close to the venue with bedrooms for us all to have privacy. The boy and girls (just one boy, brave fellow!) argued all the time about trivialities and I was wishing myself anywhere but there! Our seats in the Rexall Place were so high up; each time we needed to use the restrooms or eat we had to climb down or up a very steep stone stairway. I found it exhausting and counted the days and hours until we went home! I had a problem with my right eye, and only had vision out of half the lens so this did not help my balance on the stairs much. On the Sunday morning at the closing service the speaker (Mike Pilavachi) asked anyone who needed healing to stand! Gordon kept prompting me to stand but I refused, this was for the kids! Then as other adult leaders stood, I felt I should as well. The speaker, Mike asked all the youth around each person standing, to lay hands on them and pray for their healing. As I stood there covered in the hands of the youth who had argued and bickered for the entire time of our stay in Edmonton, I was not feeling very gracious towards them. Then I felt a peculiar sensation in my right eye as though a curtain was being pulled open across the lens and as I opened my eye, I found I could see perfectly. Yet another experience of God to humble me and emphasize it is never about 'me' or 'us' only ever according to His timing and purpose and will! Will I ever learn!!? I went home with more graciousness than I came with and joy and thanksgiving for all young people who are able to take God at His word.

As time moved on our little church was too small with the increase in congregation and we needed some additional touches like a washroom etc. It all came to a head when the Fire Marshall made an inspection as he did of all public buildings and scared the Parish Council with his follow up report. The recommendations in his report, some mandatory and some not but still sensible, caused a sharp intake of breath at the financial viability of embracing this undertaking. We were a mission parish because we needed financial support to exist, how could we possibly raise the $200,000 required? It sounded totally out of reach and ridiculous to even contemplate. God had another agenda, but we did not know this at the beginning. As I wrestled with the enormity of how we could raise such a huge sum of money, I wondered if this wasn't a ruse of the enemy to divert our attention away from bringing the Gospel to those who needed to hear it. I went into prayer mode and asked those in our church family who prayed with devotion, to join with me in this prayer quest to discover God's heart in regard to raising the funds. We all discerned that if God was in this building program to save our church building from closure then the money would come easily and quickly. If God was on our side in this the money would miraculously come. If it trickled in in bits and pieces, then we should stop trying. I and others folded over 200 hundred letters asking for financial support mailed to organizations, foundations and businesses both local, in the Territories and all across Canada. We sat back and waited! One of the Band Chief's came forward to offer to fundraise on our behalf and she raised over $60,000. Then the cheques began to arrive in the mail; several for $1000.00; several for $5,000 and others for $10,000 and more. The total kept rising and everyone was amazed. We had our answer; God was in partnership with us on this enterprise for sure! The remaining thousands of dollars were donated and pledged by generous local businesses and church donations. This was such a lesson for us all in the town. When you move in tandem with God the path is easy but try to go against Him and the going gets tough. Building commenced the very next year once the snow melted and our little church grew somewhat bigger, but importantly gained a large sanctuary, insulation, new siding and a washroom plus new storm windows, beautiful cedar wood dovetailed ceiling and new roof. St John's looked so handsome and passed all the Fire Marshall's recommendations. We could now flex our spiritual muscles with room to spare for wheelchairs and baby strollers. How we all rejoiced at the abundance of our Lord. Our Bishop Andrew Atagataluk was thrilled to sanctify the new building with us.

We had our personal challenges whilst serving up in the north with illness that had me in Yellowknife hospital for a while on two occasions and heartache when Jonah told us him and his wife were divorcing. He and I spent hours on the phone as I tried to counsel him to work things out, especially since they had our beautiful little granddaughter, who would want both her parents to be there to guide her. Sadly, we had to come to that place of acceptance as the decision had to be theirs and not ours. Jonah has since found happiness with his new lovely wife and their gorgeous young sons but always his daughter is important and firmly in his heart. Our ex-daughter in law has become a dear friend and is our 'daughter in Christ'; we love it when we see her and catch up with her news. Life is not easy and Jesus never promised us that, but He does promise to be always with us and eases our burdens when they seem too heavy for us. One cannot look back over choices made in another time and place, we can only live in the present and take today as the precious gift it is and fill it with as much goodness as we can do. In this way we lay our foundation for tomorrow that it shall be built on today's good works and our faith in God.

The years passed so quickly and as 2011 started, Gordon and I felt restlessness come into our lives; it seemed we were to prepare for a change after all this time in this place.

In 2002, we had begun to think of buying a home in Canada, a place that would belong to us; somewhere we could retire to and enjoy for vacations until that time came. I had visited Prince Edward Island many times with Jonah when he was small. It was so beautiful and safe, easy to get about and the folks always so pleased to welcome visitors. At times I would say how much I wished we could retire to a place like that. One day whilst we lived up north in Canada, Gordon had been browsing the Realtors' listings on Prince Edward Island and called me to look on the computer at this house he had found! It was most attractive and I loved it on first sight. I instantly saw the same potential Gordon did. It was in a rural setting with a large yard of the greenest grass with lovely well-established trees and shrubs. The house looked old rather than modern, yet large with two main floors and an attic and a basement. On enquiring further, we found it was about 100 years old and built during the times of the Fox fur trade, so called a Fox House. It needed some renovations but that would be part of the fun and joy of building up our very own Canadian home. The sale went through easily and in April 2003 we took the keys of our own property! Over the intervening years we went back and forth when we could (it was a long trip to get there from Fort Smith) and slowly the renos' happened as we could afford them.

Here we are now in 2011 on the verge of making a decision to retire and move east for good. It seemed so easy at first, but then doubts set in; could we bring ourselves to leave this town which had become home to us and where we had so many friends and interests. All the children I had baptized when young, I had hoped to one day see graduated and then maybe married! It broke our hearts to contemplate departing from them all; how could we say goodbye? We considered every angle, Gordon staying on here working for a while and I would retire from the Diocese and travel between east and north. That made no economic sense, so we easily dismissed that choice. At the end of the day, it all seemed decided for us. The clergy son of a congregant applied for my position and was selected, so I could retire with no qualms about leaving them without a minister. Gordon felt ready to slow down and we made our decision to leave on July 1st, 2012.

In looking back over all my years of ministry in parishes, prisons, one on one pastoring and preaching to large numbers and small, I have certainly been sent out among all nations especially in the prisons which housed men from all over the world and can hope I have been faithful in trying to make new disciples for Christ. I have baptized quite a few and spoken to them about obeying His commandments *'to love the Lord Your God with everything you are and to love your neighbour as Christ loves you.' (paraphrased).* I can only keep praying that each one of them made a righteous decision to follow Him and their hearts are full of His love today.

Chapter 9

"Your sons and daughters will prophesy, your old men will dream dreams, your young men will see visions. Even on my servants both men and women, I will pour out my Spirit in those days."

-Joel 2: 28-29; NIV

God chooses how He will communicate with us, and He has many methods to choose from. Angels are a popular choice when the Lord needs a messenger to make an attention gaining proclamation. Or through a divine outpouring of His Holy Spirit, He also takes what is very human and uses it to speak His purpose into our hearts such as dreams, seeing visions and then he commands some humans to speak His message to others, what the bible calls prophesying. So many forms of communication yet still we doubt such things and try to explain away any hint of divine connection and communication. One reason may be because the receiving of the divine communication and the confirmation of its content and context can be years even decades or millennia apart. Remember the little girl far away in Kenya sensing a numinous nudging to attend a Christian worship service even when she had no experience of such a thing and the **'prophesy' spoken to her by the minister?** That would take almost 25 years to come to be when the girl now a wife and mother had her **'ah hah! moment'** and the past caught up with her, in the present day. That of course was me and the pieces of this puzzle called my life are still being put into place but one day the whole picture will be finished once I reach that heavenly shore. The Master Weaver, our amazing Creator God will reveal the finished rug of all that is my life. All my failings, mishaps and mistakes will be redeemed and restored into perfection by Him. Remember the strange vision or dream I had over 15 years before we came to Canada of Gordon ministering as an evangelist and I was pastoring the sick and the wounded and the dying. In the background was a large white building set upon the greenest grass I had ever seen. When I first viewed our house on Prince Edward Island I experienced a vivid flash back, seeing before me the large white house set in the greenest garden and here Gordon and I would come to minister together as God intended, each of us using our specific gifts of grace. As St Paul writes "Now I see through a glass dimly, but one day shall see clearly" (paraphrased). I saw so clearly before me what the Lord had teasingly and tantalizingly shared to encourage and sustain us as we journeyed onwards, with still no idea of how it would unfold.

On Canada Day, Sunday July 1st, 2012, the heavens opened upon Fort Smith as we left for the final time on the flight to Edmonton. The rectory had been scrubbed clean, all our personal effects packed up and taken by the removal company and how were we? I was numb, as though this final departure was only a dream and I would awake to take the Sunday service at St John's as I did each Sunday morning. I could not come to the realization that this was goodbye. All the Lay Leaders had come to wish us bon voyage and I could hardly find thoughts to say to them. These beloved people with whom I had shared eleven years of worship and Bible study, how does one say farewell to such an important chunk of all our lives? I have very little recollection of us boarding the plane or the flight south. It seems I finally "woke up" on the long drive west to Banff our first stop as we drove across the Rockies. It took me a year to come to terms with leaving the north and we both still deeply miss the life we enjoyed and our many friends.

We benefited from the lovely trip enjoying stunning scenery mile after mile and eventually arrived a week later in Vancouver for our Alaska cruise. We found ourselves unbelievably blessed with an upgrade to a luxurious suite on the ship and this second chance taking a cruise up through the Inside Passage was to be memorable. No illness this time to mar our excitement as the British Columbia coast and Queen Charlotte Islands slipped by as we serenely sailed along. The half a day in Glacier Bay was the high spot for us; as we watched huge chunks of ice, the size of freight trains, 'calving' or splitting away for the edge of the glacier with the sound of a huge bomb detonating. Each port had its own beauty and interests and we were so thankful for this opportunity to have this worthwhile memorable cruise experience. On our return seven days later, we were to fly from Vancouver across the breadth of Canada to the east coast where our new life waited to begin. Sacha also waited for us with our friend Kate in Nova Scotia, but neither was at all keen on being parted and so with some tears on our part we left Sacha with Kate, knowing she would be very well looked after. In fact, Sacha adopted Kate's elderly parents and brought them much joy, so it was a really good decision if hard for us. In the way our life unfolded, it was good that Sacha had settled with Kate and her family. We had come to Prince Edward Island prepared for retirement and began to make our own house our new home. It was good to think we would not have to close up the house after a three week stay and not return for months at a time. We enjoyed having time with our close neighbours who had kindly kept a watchful eye on our place for us. Slowly we met new people, as we adapted to living at a slower pace. At times we asked ourselves how would we fill our days and how difficult it might be to make new friends now neither of us had any sort of community role. The Lord of course had everything in hand but reveals very little until His timing is perfect. It was an exceptionally hot and humid summer I recall and we spent much time in the garden trying to restore it from years of neglect with us living so far away. We had some visitors from the north who had journeyed across Canada and we loved the updates of news. Our sweet son Jonah flew from England and helped his Dad with the heavy chores that were beyond my capabilities. All in all, it was a happy relaxing summer time. Perhaps I should have known our God in Christ was up to something, but I truly thought retirement had come to stay and we would rest up.

Prince Edward Island has more churches per square kilometre than anywhere else we have lived or visited! With newfound freedom, we had enjoyed sampling other denominations' worship styles on a Sunday and found an exceptionally warm welcome at the local Baptist church. We have remained firm friends with the dear couple who pastored at that time. After a while, I was ready to attend the nearest Anglican church, up until now, I could not bring myself to have any reminders of what I had left behind in Fort Smith! This was to be the day we met the Anglican minister and his wife of our local parish and they welcomed us warmly. Reverend Andrew told me he had been taking care of the Parish of Port Hill (next door parish) but was finding leading two parishes very tiring! Over the weeks, he began to drop hints that the Diocesan Bishop was hoping I would agree to take on the Parish of Port Hill, part-time! It took me many hours of praying and reflecting if I had enough energy to begin again in a new parish, and lead three churches part-time. They deserved my very best no half measures were ever good enough in ministry, but what could I honestly achieve in such few hours each week? Once again God used situations, conversations and meeting folks to convince me this was His will and I needed to say yes! It helped that the rectory was also a large white building set upon very green grass! This vision was following us around it seemed to make sure we knew we were in the right place!! The peculiar way of the Anglican procedures went into play as I began to take services in the parish yet was not able to tell them that I would be coming as their new rector. They all knew and I knew I would be, but I was not permitted to speak of this until the bishop had completed whatever bishop's needed to do. On January 1st, 2013, I formally began employment as the rector of the Parish of Port Hill. It had served me well to have had the weeks prior to get to know a little of the quirks and unique qualities of the parish and to discover the differences between each of the three congregations. I was not encouraged at the sense of disunity between them and yet thankfully some felt they were supposed to be united as one parish. The parish finances could not afford a fulltime rector hence my part time status yet appreciated not only having me but also gaining the ministry of Gordon as a deacon. BUY ONE GET ONE!! Over the intervening years Gordon has more than proved his worth, standing in for me when I have been ill or away and also assisting with taking services for other denominations when they had a need. The Parish have more than shown their appreciation for the additional hours I offer in numerous ways and I thank them for this generosity. My proven method in each new parish or place of ministry is to listen and learn for the first six months and never to change or question anything until I have a good sense of what is going on above and below the 'water line'. By the end of the six months, I felt accepted and part of this warm rural family of hard working folks. They expressed concern as to whether the rectory was warm enough for us during a very cold January and February and suspecting our truthful answer would be no it is not, quickly sought to remedy this. We had our own home about 45 kilometres away and now had to furnish this huge rectory, buying the minimum of items to make ourselves comfortable.

The first year passed quickly and parish life settled into a rhythm that was acceptable for everyone. The community slowly opened up to us being here as they got to know us, mainly through funerals and ecumenical events. As I write, it is hard to believe this is the fifth year of ministry in this place. God has once again blessed us with more years of service just when we thought we had ended our time of usefulness. The Parish has become 'home' and the people warm, loving friends who are genuine and helpful as one would expect family to be. Only God knows the years of service we have left but this has all been pure joy, albeit hard work sometimes. I have been so privileged to conduct many wonderful weddings and countless baptisms where the grace of God is tangible and the Spirit of God radiates from faces and hearts. Funerals have always been for me such meaningful times of ministering when the truth of God and our dependence upon Him cannot be denied.

It has been in this place as the years have passed that I remember more vividly those *'whispers'* when I was so young and ignorant. Imagine what I could have missed if I had ignored the prompting, had my parents been more vigilant in monitoring my movements or if I had been a nervous child too afraid to venture far on my own? I thank God for who I am and even for all I experienced, both negative and positive, as it has made me into the woman I am today. I am far off being perfect, yet with all my soul, my mind, my body and my strength I know my God as far as I can say that truthfully and I thank Him daily for calling me by name. There have been some 'dark nights of the soul' for me where I wrestled and thankfully found my faith restored and strengthened. I have met people who have caused me to question God, both inside and outside His church. Thankfully I have also met people who have affirmed God's presence for me over and over again and these are my angels in human form, to which I offer my deepest thanks and gratitude. It has been in the trying times, the times of severe illness and tragedy that have taught me the most about the nature of God, about life and about faith and I thank God for each of them and for giving me the strength to persevere and not give up or run away; although I have been tempted often to do just that. Sometimes it seems I have lived many lifetimes and the years have raced past. Our sons are wonderful husbands and fathers of our delightful grandchildren. My dearest Gordon has been with me for over fifty years of this journey; in truth it is **our** journey, very much a team effort and much of it is because he graciously set me free and made sacrifices of all kinds so I could follow my studies and follow the Lord's direction. God has graciously teamed with Gordon so together they have been my constant guides and protectors, encouragers and mediators, my wisdom and my heart and I thank you with all that I am. I pay tribute to all who deserve to be included in my dedication of this book, the numerous I could not name. You all played a role in shaping me and encouraging me enough to get me here today and I thank you for your patience, trust, kindness and friendship which energized me to continue.

Chapter 10

'Everything that happens within us, every thought, every act of will, has cosmic repercussions, and effects all creation, for better, for worse, for richer, for poorer.'

-Gerald W. Hughes from 'God, Where Are You?'[1]

I have gotten so much inspiration and wisdom reading Gerard W. Hughes's books: The God of Surprises; God of Compassion; God, Where are You? and so was delighted to briefly meet Gerard in the UK in person as I purchased the latter book and have him sign it. I must be slow to understand some things as it is only now as I read his inscription again that I get it! This is what he wrote **"For Kathleen, 'God Where Are You'? Whenever and wherever Kathleen happens to be"!** Having written my story of my life journey (so far) I now understand God is always when and wherever we happen to be. There was never a time or a place He wasn't. Perhaps God is whispering to you and you refuse to hear Him or recognize Him? I have had the adventure of my life because I heard Him quietly, persistently getting my attention and I dared to seek Him and respond.

Books have always been an inspiration to me across all genres but the following especially stand out and my journey would not be complete without some mention:

'God of Surprises' by Gerard W. Hughes.

---
[1] Hughes Gerard W : God, Where Are You? Page 201

'God, Where are You'? by Gerard W. Hughes
'City of Joy' by Dominique Lapierre
'I heard The Owl Call My Name' by Margaret Craven
'The Way of the Paradox' by Cyprian Smith
'The Road Less Travelled' by Scott Peck
'Quarks, Chaos and Christianity' by John Polkinghorne

As I conclude this final chapter of my life journey so far, I am going to very briefly touch on the above books in an attempt to draw together the many strands of my life and all I have gained thus far. I write this in full and certain knowledge that I have much more to learn and some strands will refuse to be neatened away. Life is always messy and provocative and generally not at all in sympathy with our neat and tidy plans.

I want to begin with the only book you may find at odds with the rest, being wholly secular; 'City of Joy'[2]; this book has to be included because it blew open my mind; shook me up and widened my narrow horizons; It was not just a breath rather a hurricane of fresh air that gifted me with a new optimism and joy for our world! I had the pleasure of accompanying my husband on a business trip to Mumbai in 1987. The visit left a positive lasting impression upon me as I met some of its gracious and gentle inhabitants who taught me the value of life is beyond any material value of anyone 'thing'. Most of the city dwellers have very little in the way of material things but were rich beyond belief in joy, optimism, sharing and appreciations for life. In a conversation on this very subject a dear man, an Indian tailor whilst measuring me for a garment urged me to read the book 'City of Joy'. He became so delighted when I said I would

---

[2] City of Joy, Lapierre D.: France, Arrow, 1985

love to read it and rushed off to a nearby little kiosk returning with a copy of the book which he presented to me as a gift, I have it still to this day and it has been very well read! Within its pages I could clearly see God at work. You may have seen the movie? The book however is a must read! It is set in the very worst slums of Calcutta, slums inhumane in every description yet home to the happiest, most generous and gracious people on earth. The slums are called Anand Nagar or City of Joy and as you read the book you find out how true this is. As I began to find my way in faith in Christ, I encountered a problem. My problem was about all the amazing Godly people who do not fit neatly into Christianity as many tightly define it. Then I read this book and the blinkers fell from my eyes as I finally could see further and understand that God really did so love the whole world and not just the little bits that were considered by others to be correctly religious or those who tidily fit into the manmade institution of Christendom as parts of humanity defined it. Slum dwellers, the poorest of the poor, many so cruelly disfigured with leprosy taught me the greatest lesson of my life presenting more Christ like qualities than I can ever hope to have. In the pages of this book, I saw true Christ-like generosity being shared. Generosity isn't about one wealthy soul helping out another it is when one who has absolutely nothing still finds it possible to share with another. God's Spirit breathed out of the pages and characters and this book redefined holiness and the sacred for me, another major milestone on my journey of faith. It equipped me to recognize the sacred and holy among the degenerate prison population when I began ministry within the walls; and to respond to all I met with respect upholding their God given value and worth, not to focus on their crime. Some readers may be uncomfortable with this view, but I stand firm and ask that you read the book again and again with an open mind until God is revealed to you in all His generous and gracious holiness. I was reminded of this book over and over again as I worked within the Prison Service listening to those who many had denounced as 'not worthy' yet I held fast to the truth that God so loves this entire world and all His created beings that none should be denounced or judged prematurely for that will be for God alone on the final Day of Judgement. Jesus taught that the wheat and the weeds be left to grow together, as human hearts cannot rightly discern one from another. How blessed I have been to witness God at work in many outwardly an unworthy heart, my own included. Where would I be today if I had been denounced by anyone as unworthy or ill-prepared for God? Following on in this theme Gerard Hughes in 'God, Where are You?' writes as the Bible also records that the Spirit of God is a Spirit of truth, justice and peace, a Spirit of Unity that embraces all creation. God is always greater than any Church, any religion. Our God is a holy God, who transcends everything and is always beyond the grasp of our minds and our imaginings. He is beyond the walls we erect to keep out the undesirables, standing with them, with acceptance and love. If we truly believe our God created all things, would He then ostracize those who may not fit our manmade religious systems? John the Evangelist seems to get this when he writes:

1 John 4;7 "Dear friends, let us love one another, for love comes from God. Everyone who loves has been born of God and knows God." NIV

I love the words in The Apocrypha, in Wisdom scripture chapter 11: 24,

"Yes you love all that exists, you hold nothing you have made in abhorrence, for had you hated anything you would not have formed it. And how, if you had not willed it, could a thing persist ... You spare all things because all things Lord, are yours lover of life, you whose imperishable breath is in all. Wisdom 11: 24-12:1 REB

Margaret Craven weaves this theme within her wonderful book "I Heard the Owl call My Name"[3]. She writes of a priest who is sent by his bishop to serve in a small aboriginal community in an isolated part of British Columbia. Unknown to the young priest he is dying. Yet among the Aboriginals in the village of Kingcome, he learns enough about life to be ready to die. The story brings out his humility and mercy among a people who have not much care for God and prefer to follow their cultural ways. This priest loves them anyway as God does and he eventually shows them God's heart, through his own loving, humble example. It is only when he hears the legend of the owl, he knows his life is ending. However, he dies in peace leaving behind a legacy of faith born out of his gracious love for the people and them for him.

This world is crying out to be loved. I often pray for people unknown to me the violent men and women everywhere who practise such hatred and sow seeds of terrible destruction that they be saved by God's redeeming love. Are some created evil; I cannot believe this as God cannot look upon anything evil; this line of thinking provokes constructive, thoughtful responses and is not the purpose of this book. I ask you to reflect on this

---

[3] Craven, I Heard the Owl Call My Name: Toronto, Clark Irwin, 1967

quote from the back cover of Gerard Hughes book 'God of Compassion'[4]

> *'God is in everyone and in all things, and God is a God of love, of compassion, and of justice. All creation is a sacrament of God, a sign of God's presence. Everyone and everything is sacred.'*

The more we understand the less we know and so we arrive at the point of admitting that following God is "The Way of The Paradox"[5] to use Meister Eckhart's title. I have read this compact inspirational book on spiritual life many times, each reading resulting in a new discovery of another spiritual gem. Quoting from these final three books on my list, all sharing the theme of paradox; I start with Cyprian Smith's translation of Meister Eckhart's work, written in German in 1936. I wish to draw attention to the chapter of 'The Voice of God' page 64 as it was God's whispered voice that originally motivated my discovery of God. Here is written what the spiritual life at its deepest is all about; not merely believing in God, or even worshiping Him, but *knowing God* as in *dwelling in Him*. We no longer 'follow' Him but we enter into a full relationship with Him through Christ in every sense. If you wish to take this understanding further (and it is worthwhile) read the whole book or at the very least the whole chapter. *Living in Christ* affects our attitude to the world around us, all people and things. We begin to see the world as God sees it and this promotes the huge question of 'How does God see the world?' Here is where we encounter extraordinary paradox as Eckhart keeps us

---

[4] Hughes, God of Compassion; Great Britain, Hodder & Stoughton, 1998
[5] Smith C, Meister Eckhart 'The Way of The Paradox', London, Dalton, Longman & Todd, 1987

focused on the tensions between opposites, pleasure and pain; success and failure; light and dark; life and death; etc., ultimately all one in God.

Scott Peck in 'The Road Less Travelled"[6], also writes of paradox. In his chapter on **"The Welcoming of Grace'** [7] he says that it is our choice whether or not we are blessed by God's Grace which is correct surely as we all have freedom of will to choose all things for ourselves? Yet at the same time grace doesn't wait for us to grasp it, it comes to us and often surprises us when we least expect it. This has been my experience over and over again on my life journey. How we resolve this paradox, Peck says, we can't. However, we can prepare ourselves to become fertile spiritual ground so as to be welcoming to God's Spirit, so in this way we are open to the gift of grace for when it arrives and surprises us. Buddha found enlightenment only when he stopped seeking it. In my life grace has found me at times I have not been seeking or expecting such a gift. Humility plays a role here for those who know they deserve nothing find abundance of joy through grace. Those who earnestly feel they deserve God to fill them are often disappointed. I use the following often in preaching or teaching *'God can only fill empty hands and full hearts.* When we cry out to Him holding up full hands and empty hearts, what we already have has to be sufficient. Contemplating paradox in our faith is not to be feared or avoided for out of such exercise we develop spiritual muscle and courage and deepen our roots in Christ our Saviour.

I come to my final book choice, perhaps the ultimate paradox of all, belief in God and in science! I strongly recommend John

---

[6] The Road Less Travelled, Peck S; London, Arrow, 1978
[7] Peck, page 328 onwards

C. Polkingthorne, an internationally known Anglian priest and physicist who writes with ease and wisdom of the logical friendship between science and religion. In his book **"Quarks, Chaos and Christianity"**[8] he draws on discoveries made in atomic physics to make credible claims of Christianity, giving an answer to the question: can a scientist believe in God? He writes science and religion are intellectual cousins under the skin. In my own secular education, I followed a scientific, analytical path and still uphold science alongside the theological path. Each has a part in the great human endeavour searching for belief and understanding of our Universe. Neither one is exclusive of the other. We need both insights as Polkinghtorne attests to understand religion and science properly. Faith is a leap, but into the light not into the dark. Science illuminates the shape and structure of what we find while theology informs the manner of its becoming.

> *'The world in which we live is multi layered in the richness of its reality. One of the attractions of the religious account is that, in seeing the will and nature of the Creator underlying and unifying the varieties of human experience, it makes this richness more intelligible. Our scientific explorations are insights into the rational order with which God has endowed this universe. Our experiences of beauty are a sharing in His joy in creation. Our moral perceptions are intuitions of His good and perfect will. Our religious experiences are encounters of His hidden presence. Such a view is whole and satisfying;*

---

[8] Polkingthorne, John; Quarks, Chaos & Christianity, London; SPCK Triangle;1994

it has the ring of truth about it. Who are we? We are God's creatures."[9]

So my journey comes to a natural 'way station' and this is where you leave me to continue my journey for however long I am called to continue, and you continue your own journey. Thank you, for coming along, this far.

My life story began with my childlike response to 'whispers' or nudges deep within trying to gain my attention, since then my life has been years of faltering, stumbling steps to understand what this is all about. I am overawed that God should have any interest in me, yet I am not surprised because his nature is to have interest in each one of us. You are of great interest to your heavenly Father. If you have read this book seeking some direction or answers for yourself, I pray you find some hope and inspiration. God has myriad, different responses for each one of us but we can take heart and encouragement from another's blessings. If your blessings are not the same as mine, rejoice for they will be perfect for your life. Nobody is ever born as a result of a 'mistake'! God calls each one into being, born in the perfection of his love and desires to see us fulfil our destiny. I have made quite a mess of seeking to fulfil mine and yet I am learning that my heavenly Father never loses patience with me and is weaving all my messes, all my errors and failures into an original masterpiece; beautiful, and perfect as my unique life picture. Not because I am especially commendable, but all because our God is special and I thank Him that I am His child, His daughter, called by His Grace. My

---

[9] Polkingthorne, Chapter " Who Are We? , page 61

life has been truly blessed and I wouldn't have missed it for the world!

THE END

Afterword

It has been an emotional roller coaster writing this book. Many memories had lain hidden for decades and chose this time to reveal themselves in the text. Each time I sat down at the computer I never had any plan of what would appear on the page, the words came *unbidden as though they were subconsciously being pushed* up onto the page and I think they were. This book has lain dormant for years inside me and now is the time to share what God has revealed in my life for some purpose I know not! All I do know is that through Christ my life is now in way better shape than it was. I shall never stop thanking Him for finding me and persevering in tutoring me in His purpose for my life. Do not model yourself on me, it is important that you look always to God and seek what He wishes for **your life**.

My husband encouraged me to begin writing and as usual he turned out to be right! I also thank Author's Tranquility Press for making the publication possible and for all the advice and expertise they gave me.

Go in the peace of Christ and serve Him.

Glossary

East African language

SWAHILI	ENGLISH
Chumbe Kikuyu	man's name
Hujambo	Hello
Kwahari	Goodbye
Memsahib	Female (term of respect)
Mau Mau Kikuyu	Guerrilla army
Masai	East African tribe
Uhuru	Independence
Ngong Hills	Knuckle Hills

(All copyright of the content of this manuscript belongs solely to Ann Kathleen Bush and may not be copied or quoted or otherwise used without her written permission.)

About the Author

After leaving school in East Africa, my parents permitted me to fly to the United Kingdom so I could train in Aviation. I was excited to be out in the world and worked hard in my first career. During this time, I met and married my life partner. We share two sons and five wonderful grandchildren. I was also moving and growing in a religious sense, God was still 'whispering 'to me in my heart. Some years later, I found myself within Christ Church, Oxford being ordained into Anglican ministry by the then Bishop of Oxford.

This day was to be a new beginning as I left aviation and started on an exciting part of my journey as a pastor and priest, that would take us to other continents to meet wonderful new friends.

My family as not privileged, but very ordinary, yet I was blessed to meet many extraordinary people, have adventures and incredible experiences.

CPSIA information can be obtained
at www.ICGtesting.com
Printed in the USA
BVHW082228070223
658049BV00005B/881